GOOD
BAD GUY
3

GOOD GUN
BAD GUY
3

Exposing Anti-Gun Politics

By Dan Wos

WOSCORP PUBLISHING
SARATOGA SPRINGS, NY

Good Gun Bad Guy 3

First Edition Library of Congress Cataloging-in-Publication Data

Good Gun Bad Guy 3 | Daniel J. Wos – 1st ed.

Paperback
ISBN-13: 978-0-692-70855-2
ISBN-10: 0692708553
Hardcover:
ISBN-13: 978-0-578-61604-9
ISBN-10: 0578616049

Edited by Bill Dolan
Foreword by Jan Morgan
Foreword by Erich Pratt
Cover design by Dan Wos

WosCorp Publishing
PO BOX 3331
Saratoga Springs, NY 12866
www.goodgunbadguy.com

Printed in the United States of America

10 9 8 7 6 5 4 3 2

For The American Gun Owner

"For it is a truth, which the experience of ages has attested, that the people are always most in danger when the means of injuring their rights are in the possession of those of whom they entertain the least suspicion."

- Alexander Hamilton, *Federalist No. 25*, December 21, 1787

"All political power comes from the barrel of a gun. The communist party must command all the guns, that way, no guns can ever be used to command the party."

- Mao Tse Tung

This year will go down in history. For the first time, a civilized nation has full gun registration! Our streets will be safer, our police more efficient and the world will follow our lead into the future!

- Adolf Hitler, passing of the German Weapons Act 1935

"I stand in support of this common-sense legislation to license everyone who wishes to purchase a gun. I also believe that every new handgun sale or transfer should be registered in a national registry."

- Hillary Clinton

TABLE OF CONTENTS

Good Gun Bad Guy 3

FOREWORD

By Jan Morgan

Imagine for a moment, you are standing on the side of a boat. In the water below, you see the sharks, fiercely circling the boat in anticipation of their next meal. Your mauled friends standing behind you, (missing limbs from their own ventures into the shark infested waters), are encouraging you to jump in. They say, "it is your turn to take one for the team." That is exactly how I felt when a CNN producer left a phone message requesting I appear on the network. My friends on the 2A front insisted I accept the invite to engage in ENEMY TERRITORY. If you are a Constitutional Conservative Commentator, appearing on CNN in a debate is like jumping in the water with a bunch of hungry sharks.

Appearing on national tv as a political analyst or 2nd Amendment advocate was in my comfort zone. I had been a TV News Anchor/Reporter for decades and had become a regular on Fox News for several years. I also appeared on One America News Network, NRATV and a host of other TV and radio networks, sharing political analysis on the latest political issues, and had successfully engaged in a number of debates on the 2nd Amendment. I had even been on CNN INTERNATIONAL TV during the Republican National Convention, (as the National Spokesperson of Citizens for Trump)

The anchor for CNN International was very professional (though we disagreed on virtually everything), and she engaged with me in a civilized, intelligent, and professional manner, allowing me equal time to answer her questions and state my position. She seemed genuinely interested in trying to understand why Conservatives think the way we do. But.... CNN (NATIONAL).... was... different.

I knew I was being asked to jump in to a tank filled with sharks. I called my fellow commentator friends at NRATV and at Fox News and whined about the request, hoping JUST ONE of them would tell me I should not agree to the debate on a network referred to by our President and many on the Conservative side as "Fake News."

I hoped just one of them would say, "you have nothing to gain and everything to lose by agreeing to go on that show, on that network," and that I should not agree to it under any circumstances. That didn't happen. In fact, each person I called, including the author of this book, Dan Wos, said, "You have to do this." Others said, "You may speak the only words of truth their audience hears all day...... that is...... if they allow you to speak a complete sentence without interrupting you and speaking over you." (That is what they do at CNN if you start to say something conservative that they don't want their audience to hear, or if you are winning the debate.")

But... hey... they said.... We will be watching and cheering you on.. and praying for you that you don't lose your cool, cuss, and destroy your credibility forever on live tv. Thanks guys for the positive send off in to the shark tank. The rest is history.

CNN put me on live tv, on a show hosted by a 2nd Amendment loathing anchor, to debate a criminal defense attorney who was also a victim/survivor of the Las Vegas shooting massacre. What could possibly go wrong? I've successfully debated attorneys on national tv many times. It's easy when the United States Constitution and Bill of Rights are on your side. But imagine trying to debate gun rights on national tv against a guy who had been a victim/survivor of a recent mass shooting? That requires carefully crafted, tactful language and a level of compassion while delivering correction to his misguided thinking. I didn't want to lose the audience by appearing insensitive.

The anchor set the stage on live tv by handing him a question that allowed him to unload his grief rather than discuss the legalities of the issue at hand. He took full advantage of the hand-off she gave him. He said the fact that our nation was even discussing the latest gun rights issue made him feel "shocked, re-victimized, re-traumatized, grief stricken and in despair." He described in detail the sounds of bullets around him, the screams, how he felt in those critical moments... He talked about dodging bullets, thinking he was going to die. He vowed that if he survived, he would fight to "ban all assault weapons and any pro-gun legislation."

Then, he and the anchor turned to me, and the anchor wanted to know my feelings on the issue. After all, how could I possibly defend the right to keep and bear arms without more regulations and restrictions after hearing this poor man pour out his heart and soul about running for his life under a barrage of bullets being fired from a rifle in the hands of a mad man?

Let me pause the story to say this: I swear to you, I was thanking God for Dan Wos and his first two books, Good Gun Bad Guy 1 and 2, for preparing me for this very moment. What I learned from him in those books, was, in that moment, equivalent to being thrown weapons to fight off the sharks and a life vest to keep from drowning while shark slaying. If you have not read his first two books, you should purchase them now. The first rule of war is to know your enemy. REALLY KNOW your enemy..... not just who he is, but how he thinks, what triggers him, how he fights, what are his weapons, and what are his weaknesses. Only then can you successfully defeat him. I knew from debating far left anti-gun radicals in the past, that their arguments are emotion based and they rely on the emotion of the moment after a tragedy, to push for legislation to restrict the rights of innocent Americans because of the actions of a bad guy. Debating an actual victim who could legitimately bring all those emotions to the debate was an entirely different arena for me.

Dan's books prepared me for that moment. You will have to go on the internet to watch the debate. I also suggest you watch the video Dan Wos put together after the debate, breaking down each part, demonstrating how the left uses strategies to impact how people feel about guns to gain support for further infringements. Link to video:

https://www.youtube.com/watch?v=hiLodcI_E50&t=1s

I not only survived the two against one attack on CNN, but, I successfully managed to get a few complete sentences out (when the anchor and lawyer weren't interrupting me) about the common denominator in almost all mass shootings that no one on the left wants to talk about and that we should not eliminate rights based on feelings. I kept my composure. He did not. He actually said, "rights are what is wrong with America." That would have shocked me had I not learned something about people on the far left from Dan's books.

He says the anti-gun left actually views rights as government issued privileges to be regulated and restricted. They are more comfortable with the idea of living under heavy government control. In the final moments of my CNN adventure, the "victim/survivor" threatened me with this desperate parting shot on national tv, "the blood of the next mass shooting victims will be on YOUR hands." He might as well have said, you won Jan, because the most powerful card he could think of to play in that moment was the blame card.

Blaming and punishing good guys for the actions of bad guys is not a winning strategy. It makes as much sense as sheep removing their own teeth because the wolves attacking the herd are killing sheep with their sharp teeth. How is removing their own teeth going to make the sheep safe from wolves with teeth?

My point in sharing the CNN fiasco is this: we all, at some time or another, are standing on the side of that boat staring at the sharks. We all have people in our lives, whether its family, friends, or coworkers, who are anti-gun people. Discussing gun rights with them is as unpleasant as the thought of jumping off that boat in to shark infested water. That is why you need to read this book.

Dan Wos knows how these people think, feel, and talk about guns. He knows because he was once one of them... sort of. He was never an Anti 2nd Amendment Radical. He ran with that crowd, but because he is an intelligent man, once he began to actually think about the issue and study it to establish his own position, he saw the light and is now one of our best assets on the 2A battleground! I wrote the forewords for both of his earlier books. I did not think there was any way he could top the valuable information in his first two. Then, he sent me the manuscript for Good Gun Bad Guy 3.

It is the best yet! Read it, then join us on the front lines using what you have learned to educate Americans who have lost their way and have become comfortable with the notion that living life defenseless is perfectly normal and acceptable. Every mind you change on this issue is critical. Dan's book gives you the tools you need to transform minds from the position that "Guns kill people"... to GUNS SAVE LIVES!

Our Founding Fathers fled tyranny, fought for independence, and gave us a Constitutional Republic. LET'S MAKE SURE WE KEEP IT!

~ Jan Morgan
Analyst on Fox News
First Lady of the 2nd Amendment
National Conservative Commentator
National Director of 2A Women
NRA and State Police Certified Firearms Instructor

FOREWORD
By Erich Pratt

Kaboom. Kaboom. Kaboom.

I was treating an adult daughter and her friend with a trip to the range. My daughter is comfortable with firearms. Her friend—we'll call her Sally—was not.

I started setting up the handguns and ammunition on the tray in front of us. The shooters in the lane next to us were already firing their weapons. But this was not the "pop, pop, pop" that one would hear from a small caliber handgun.

Kaboom. Kaboom. Kaboom.

It was loud. Even with our hearing protection on, it was very loud. You could feel the percussion coming through the partition into our lane.

Kaboom. Kaboom. Kaboom.

Sally had initially been excited about her first ever trip to a gun range. But now she was growing increasingly irritable and nervous. She tried to brave it for as long as she could. But finally, she could take it no longer. Sally burst into tears and ran out of the range. My daughter followed her out, gently comforted her and eventually led her back in—roughly 15 minutes later.

Sally explained that "feeling" the percussion from the firearms near us brought back memories of the mass killings she had seen in the news. While she had never any personal interaction with firearms, it was as if she was suffering from a PTSD flashback. Sally was consumed with fear.

Let me pause the story here to point out the insightful masterpiece that Dan Wos has written. In *Good Gun, Bad Guy 3*, Dan Wos explains how the anti-gun Left brainwashes and conditions the public to fear guns.

And lest you think that the word "brainwash" is mere fearmongering from the Right, Wos will show you that gun banners readily admit this is what they're doing. Remember Eric Holder saying that, "We have to ... brainwash people into thinking about guns in a vastly different way"? You'll see that quote—and many more—in the pages that follow. Because Wos shows you the shameful techniques that gun banners will use to mold young minds into fearing guns.

Having spoken with Sally about our outing at the range, I now see that her fear of guns precisely fits with the indoctrination techniques that Wos outlines in this book. But as Wos suggests in Chapter 2, a trip to the range can be a total game changer for someone who has been conditioned to fear guns by anti-rights educators and media. For Sally, that was thankfully the case.

As we prepared to leave the gun range, Sally was all smiles—grinning from ear to ear. She even insisted that my daughter take a picture of her, posing with a .38 Smith & Wesson revolver—a gun that had a formidable "kick" for a beginner. That one afternoon helped inoculate Sally from undergoing a horrid transition that Wos describes in *Good Gun, Bad Guy 3*—where an Anti-gunner, who is scared of guns, transitions into an anti-gun Radical who pushes for restrictions upon everyone else's rights.

I met Dan Wos at a gun rights conference in Alabama. Both of us were speakers at the event, and we told the audience about our respective battles in defending our Second Amendment-protected rights.

As I listened to Dan speak that day, I remember being impressed with how well he understood the anti-gunners' thinking. But it's no wonder. He used to be one. And that's why *Good Gun, Bad Guy 3* is such a valuable resource. His conversational approach will not only help you to understand what the anti-gun Left thinks, but why they think it. Dan is putting a manual in your hands that will supply you with good arguments that will keep you from being flat-footed when you're engaging your friends and family who are anti-freedom.

I especially like that Dan grounds his entire discussion on the right to keep and bear arms by first comparing rights versus privileges. As Dan so cogently explains, privileges are something that is given by man and can be taken back. But God-given rights cannot be taken or revoked, which is why our Declaration of Independence says they are "unalienable."

Well, as Dan details in *Good Gun, Bad Guy 3*, the modern Left not only hates God, they despise the notion of God-given rights—so much so, that they will even sanction murder when it fits their narrative. Fighting against your Second Amendment-protected rights truly is, as Wos suggests, a "political religion" for the anti-rights zealots.

All that being said, Dan Wos gives the reader hope. Gun rights are advancing in this country, in tremendous leaps and bounds. He notes that as of June 2019, there are 17 states which enjoy Constitutional Carry—states where decent citizens can carry a firearm for protection without first getting a permit. This is amazing when one considers that in 2000, there was only one state (Vermont) that enjoyed permitless carry.

So use this book. Highlight it and take notes. This book is full of good analysis and statistics that will greatly empower you. As part of my job, I have spent quite a bit of time debating gun grabbers on CNN, MSNBC, and even on Fox News. Yet I have learned some great arguments from reading the third volume of the *Good Gun, Bad Guy* series.

Sun Tzu in *The Art of War* explains how important it is for one to know their enemy. Well, we have political enemies who want to disarm us. And this book will help you to better understand—and to intellectually disarm—these opponents. So when you finish this volume, make sure you get a copy of the first two books in the *Good Gun, Bad Guy* series. You won't be disappointed!

-Erich Pratt
Senior Vice President
Gun Owners of America
Twitter: @erichmpratt

EDITOR'S NOTE
By Bill Dolan

True confessions. I'm not sure I should say this publicly but I have to come clean.

I don't carry. There, I said it. It's out there, it's in black and white forever. It's embarrassing and I've kept it a dark secret for too long ...and I had to be honest about it. Now that I've said it, you know what? I don't care what paranoid sky-is-falling people say.

I've made my choice and I don't carry...an umbrella. Nope. Don't even keep a little one under the seat of the car.

When discussing my Every Day Carry (EDC) with non-carriers I've said the following many times (and I get choked up at the end every time).

"Ya' know what, I am right behind you not carrying a gun. *Of course* it isn't something everyone would want to do. And I totally understand that you'd question why someone would carry a gun ...and this may surprise you but, even though I don't leave the house without one... I know I'll never have to use it. I mean, most cops work 20 years in the business of being around criminals and never *unholster* their handgun, let alone have to fire it in a life-or-death situation...so me ever having to do so in my boring life is a long shot. I'd bet...I'd bet a year's salary that I'll never need my gun."

Here I pause to let the common ground and reasonableness sink in a bit and follow up with,

"You know what I won't bet, though? I won't bet my little girl's life. The downside's just too great."

Do I "EDC" a chest seal, decompression needle, AED, a pumper truck, and an M249 SAW? Nope. But a little Austrian insurance, spare mag and a little medical (along with a charged phone, a pointy pokey persuader, flashlight, 3/4+ tank of gas...) all seem like cheap insurance in an "oh poop" type situation.

It's not for everyone...and that's okay. Choice. Freedom. Live and let live. It's what our country (and decency) was built on. Thomas Paine probably said it best in 'Common Sense' - "March to the beat of whatever floats your boat, Bro." Or maybe that was Steve McQueen ...or Wayne Dyer. Doesn't matter.

The string-pulling Anti-2nd Amendment Radicals do their best to define the argument. They feed their impressionable Anti-Gunners focus-group-tested Orwellian Doublespeak talking points and Straw Man arguments ...and sadly, the Anti-Gunners fall for it and parrot the lies like good True Believers. "Useful Idiots" one might say. Some people just want to belong and be able to sit at the Popular Table. Unfortunately, the price of admission is truth, integrity, and the safety of the rest of us.

Dan's GGBG books peel away layers of the onion. The outer layers are the bait - the façade meant for public consumption and the persuasion of the uneducated. Inside, though, is the sinister core - and Dan exposes the motives behind the Anti-2nd Amendment Radicals' obsession with "gun control." Any student of history knows that removing the means of self-defense is a box to check for tyrants-in-waiting. It's *people-control*, they crave. Why? Because they despise you. They look down on you. They're smarter and
XX

more sophisticated than you. You...and all your self-determination and religion and respect for time-proven tradition. You...and your fingernails dirty from paying the price for sending kids to college, your WalMart shopping, soccer games, changing your own oil, not summering in the Hamptons and wintering in Aspen...your refusal to be assimilated. You are in the way. As a Japanese friend says, "Deru kugi wa utareru." (The nail that sticks up gets the hammer.) Hammer they will. They are tireless in marginalizing and demonizing the concept of gun ownership in the media, lying about the 2nd Amendment in the government ("public") schools, and pour millions of dollars into lobbying and elections. It's a battle on all fronts but 'Good Gun Bad Guy' lays out their intentions and deceptions so we can be prepared.

In a July 2014 Rolling Stone interview, NannyState Know It All Hypocrite Mr. Bloomberg said,

"And if you want to have a gun in your house, I think you're pretty stupid – particularly if you have kids – but I guess you have a right to do that."

"I think you're pretty stupid."
"I guess you have a right."

Mike doesn't want to get rid of guns. He wants to get rid of "stupid" people's guns - *your* guns. He doesn't "guess" if *he* has a right. He *knows* he has a right. Are you wondering if his 17 person security detail carries those Kentucky rifles for which the 2nd Amendment was written? Surely his silverbacks don't carry the one purpose: made-for-killing weapons-of-war ...with *gasp* detachable magazines ...and hold *gulp* more than 7 rounds.

Read Dan's newest 'Good Gun Bad Guy 3' and see exactly what the fight is about - our lives. As I said, we can now be prepared for their deceptive tactics. Should we absolutely have to meet a debate head on, facts and Natural Law is on our side. But the best tactic is to *not be there*: don't accept the premise that this is about pistol grips, waiting periods or 30 round magazines. We get buried in the minutia by arguing details - all the while we're back on our heels in defense-mode. *There is no reason a rational, peaceful adult should not have the means to preserve his or her most basic property - him/herself.* Period. There is no house, marriage, dream, productivity, or purpose without *being*. All else is ancillary.

Utopia is not an option. "Cain used a rock" was a very effective meme going around this year. The tag line was "The object isn't what God held accountable." Just because the grocery stores are stocked, we have indoor plumbing and iPhones doesn't mean human nature has changed. The elites and the NPR-listening, purple-crystal-meditating ostriches would have you believe otherwise (and call you a delusional throwback to boot).

I've done the math and made my choice: getting a little wet in the rain I can deal with. Being helpless should any harm come to that little princess of mine? Not an option.

~Bill Dolan
November 2019

PREFACE

There's an evil game being played and the prize is power. Power over society, which really means control of as many people as possible. Now, I know what you're thinking. "This is crazy talk. I live in America where the people are free." I understand this isn't Nazi Germany. We have different guidelines in America. We have a Constitution that directs the flow of government processes and structures the way in which it functions. We also have an additional document created as an addendum which outlines that government's boundaries with regard to the citizens of America. It's called the Bill of Rights and it was written later and attached to the Constitution to remind those in power, who they actually work for. Why do you think our Founders felt the need to create these guidelines? Could it be, they understood the tendencies of people? Don't forget, they had already experienced being on the wrong end of power. They understood that it was a very demoralizing position to be in. They also understood that those who had power seemed to lose compassion for those whom they controlled.

Does the need to control society change depending on where we live in the world? We may forget that just because we live in America, it doesn't necessarily mean that some among us wouldn't love to control the actions of everyone. If you took Stalin and changed his geographic location, would he have suddenly developed different psychological tendencies?

No, I'm not a conspiracy theorist. I'm a guy who grew up in the suburbs of upstate New York and had a relatively average middle class experience. All I really wanted to do was play guitar and make my own choices, but as I got older, I started to see some very distinctive patterns among my fellow man. Patterns that were hard to deny. I started to recognize a hierarchy of power forming, regardless of the guidelines that were created to prevent it. It almost seems like an instinctive need to control others out of a fear of a possible negative outcome. It could be the notion that with control over society, those in control would be able to reap financial rewards, which may also be driven by fear. Fear of being controlled themselves. If the latter is true, it would indicate that those seeking power understand the tendencies of man and really just want to get out in front of it. Maybe this need for control was always there and it just took me some time to recognize it. It's not a passion for power exclusively driven by the men in our society either, because if you look, you'll see women with the same incessant hunger for it as well. Oftentimes in America, the idea that we live in a patriarchal society is pushed as a way to re-direct the focus and prevent people from seeing that the need to control comes in both sexes.

What really causes people to seek control? I'm not necessarily talking about control over large portions of society. Let's bring it down to a local level. What controls have you set in place for your own family? Do you have controls, rules or boundaries for your children? Why? What are you so afraid of that causes you to want to control the environment within which they live? Is it for their own safety? What about controlling violent criminals? We created prisons for them. Is that for their own safety? My guess is that you like the idea of controlling violent criminals because you are looking out for your *own* safety. Control or power over others always has a self-serving component. The need for control comes from a fear of an imagined outcome and always benefits those seeking it. Our Founding Fathers knew, that given the ability, some people would abuse their power and put themselves at the top of the hierarchical food chain to keep the control all to themselves. They knew people would do this because they knew that the need for control is inherent. Remember, they just got done taking control from the British. They knew that if they did not preserve that power, someone else would come along and control them. So they created territorial boundaries and written guidelines for anyone who stepped foot inside. They never wanted future generations to go through the hell that they went through. They were very thoughtful in their messaging to people who would come along hundreds of years later. They did not want anything they said to be misunderstood.

So why was the Bill of Rights written? To remind everyone that certain human values exist and were never to be violated. It was a message to the men and women who would surely come along and try to take advantage of those who just wanted to make their own choices, raise their families and live an honest life. The most profound and insightful collection of words ever written in the Bill of Rights can be found in the 2nd Amendment. It was written out of recognition that there would be some people who would come along and try to take advantage of others. It would be a line of words that recognized the leverage firearms would be able to give good people against those with bad intentions. It would send a resounding message to everyone who wanted to be part of the American experiment in a free society, that good people will always have the leverage to protect their own lives. Good people will hold their own power. Good people will take the path they choose. It was fourteen words that would let everyone know, that the good guys have guns and it is not a topic that will be up for debate. Ever. Those words were,

"…the right of the people to keep and bear Arms, shall not be infringed."

Unfortunately, there are men and women, some who have scratched and clawed their way to power, in our government who pretend those profound words mean something else. They want desperately to convince you that those words are no longer valid or now come with stipulations. They work hard every day to create laws and policies that undermine those fourteen words for one reason. To create the illusion that your inherent right to protect yourself and freedom doesn't really exist. They see how other countries have done it. They understand how it feels to have control. They can taste the freedom that comes with being at the top of the food chain and they are afraid of those who are wise to their strategy. They will do whatever they can to restrict and regulate firearms out of the hands of good people in order to preserve their own control. Don't for a minute believe that gun-restrictions are to save lives and keep guns out of the hands of bad guys. If they were, the gun laws in America would have some effect on the bad guys. They don't, but they do affect the good guys.

While our Democrat employees work hard every day to develop new anti-gun propaganda and rhetoric, their lap dog media falls in line and you get told what you can and can't do in the process. You get positioned as the problem. If only you would give up your guns, we could all live peacefully. You and I both know why firearms are the biggest political target but let's dig into it and explore it in detail. The gun-grabbers are not going to like this. This is the stuff you are not supposed to see.

ACKNOWLEDGMENTS

Since the release of the first edition of the Good Gun Bad Guy series, I have learned that gun-owners are some of the most honorable, responsible and patriotic people on the planet. I say this because after meeting and sharing stories with people from all over the country, it is crystal clear that those who support the 2nd Amendment do it for reasons that come from a wellspring of historical knowledge, forward, generational thinking, and deep personal integrity. Gun-ownership is often tied directly to a love for America and an understanding of how important freedom really is, but most often a responsibility to preserve life; their own and the lives of those they care about.

To the contrary, it has also become clear to me, that those who oppose gun-ownership do it primarily for reasons of fear, often due to misguided political views or lack of information. Those who want guns to go away because they fear them, may have a genuine misunderstanding of guns but many seem to be unwilling or unable to see the topic of guns through a perspective that may put their current beliefs at risk. Then there are those whose intentions are for nothing other than winning the debate at all costs. They know gun-restrictions put good people in danger and they don't care because their politics define their beliefs and they'll fight to the death to defend them – logic, facts and morality be damned.

The acknowledgments here, are of the people who never stop fighting, and will always defend our 2nd Amendment in the face of some of the most ruthless among the anti-gun crowd.

Special thanks to Jan Morgan for your support, friendship and unwavering passion to defend the 2nd Amendment.

Special thanks to Bill Dolan for all the hard work you have done editing my books and keeping the message structured and focused. I know my grammar and punctuation can be... let's just say, "challenging."

To everyone who supported Good Gun Bad Guy and Good Gun Bad Guy 2 and those who speak loudly in support of the 2nd Amendment: Jan Morgan, Bill Dolan, BamaCarry, Larry Pratt, Erich Pratt, GOA, Kevin Burns, Michael Hart, KrisAnne Hall, Grant Stinchfield, Denise Petty, Cam Edwards, Cameron Gray, Cheryl and Dan Todd, Beth Alcazar, Greg Hopkins, Remso Martinez, Amanda Suffecool, Rob Suffecool, Tom Gresham, Willes Lee, Dana Loesch, Sean Hannity, Amanda Head, Rory Sauter, Julio Rivera, A.J. Rice, Fredy Riehl, Paul Arnold, Wayne LaPierre, David Keene, Mark Walters, NRA, Chris Cox, Ted Nugent, Keith Hansen, 2nd Amendment Foundation, Alan Gottlieb, Julianne Versnel, Jennifer Boehme, Charlie Cook, Sheriff David Clarke, President Donald Trump, John Lott Jr., Mark Levin, Ben Shapiro, Craig DeLuz, David Petronis, Bill Frady, Debbie Georgatos, Joyce Kaufman, Paul Harrell, Roger Henriksson, Sean Spicer, Dan Roberts ...and everyone I've had the great opportunity of getting to meet across this great country. Your stories, your families and your commitment are what makes America great...

INTRODUCTION

Every topic has its own narrative. The narrative is shaped by those who have the most influence over the topic in the public eye. Most often, the Media, Hollywood, public schools and our government drive the narrative. Sometimes for monetary reasons but often for political leverage. I have been most interested in the narrative that surrounds gun-ownership because it has been so corrupted. The anti-gun narrative puts millions of people in danger every day but somehow has managed to gain loyal support from some who live among us.

The gun narrative has been perverted by dishonest people with a selfish agenda fueled by their own fear of guns and hatred toward gun-owners. That fear and hate is the driving force behind the radical gun-grabbers. Without the ability to instill fear and hate in their supporters, they would not have the motivation needed to encourage law-makers to find more ways to restrict gun-ownership among law-abiding citizens.

Irrationally induced fear of guns and an unjust perpetually driven hatred towards gun-owners is the fuel that keeps them going. Without it, America would organically revert back to a fond appreciation of firearms. Why? Because it is in the American DNA. Guns are why we have the freedom we do and people understand that. Yes, even the anti-gun crowd… although they will never admit it. The Anti-2nd Amendment Radicals have a very difficult job; removing guns from society. … which is why they need a consistent, powerful, and persistent message. If they let up for a minute, they will lose support and momentum. That's the good news. The bad news is, they have a political party that is committed to destroying America as our Founding Fathers saw it, they have the Media on their side and they have managed to infect our school system while we weren't paying attention.

Americansocialists are no longer hiding their ugly fantasies. An unarmed society, controlled by a government they keep in power is now their mainstream platform and they are not ashamed to admit it.

I'm committed to exposing the corruption, tactics and strategies of those who manipulate the thought process of people on the topic of guns. The dishonest gun-narrative ultimately puts everyone in danger because it encourages laws that disarm good people and make them vulnerable to attacks, ultimately bringing us further from the America our Founders envisioned. We see the immediate dangers of disarmament when women are sexually attacked, children are killed in their classroom and good people are murdered because they were unable to defend themselves. Notice how the Anti-2nd Amendment Radicals never mention the possibility of defensive guns preventing such incidents, only the need for even more gun-restrictions as soon as an incident occurs. You would almost think they welcome heinous acts committed with the use of a gun to further their agenda, but that would be crazy conspiracy talk.

Until we push back on the false gun narrative, the gun grabbers will continue to create the gun narrative that *they* want to create. They will continue to recruit more anti-gun warriors and perpetuate even more fear and hatred in society. They ultimately put you in an unsafe position by making you unable to protect yourself while simultaneously encouraging violent attackers by removing any opposition. *"An armed society is a polite society"* and the gun-grabbers know this. They also know that the people who make up an "armed society" are inherently in control of their own money, efforts, decisions and destiny. That's the part they don't like.

XXX

In the pages ahead, we will talk about the strategies and tactics of the Anti-Gunners and Anti-2nd Amendment Radicals so you can see exactly what they are doing and why they are doing it. We will also discuss ways that we *real* Americans can ultimately defeat the gun-grabbers and defend the values that have always made America great. The Second Amendment is not a privilege, it's your right. Now it's our responsibility to defend it.

Good Gun Bad Guy 3

1. ANTI-GUN INDOCTRINATION

"We just have to be repetitive about this. It's not enough to have a catchy ad on a Monday and then only do it every Monday. We have to do this every day of the week and just really brainwash people into thinking about guns in a vastly different way."
– Eric Holder

We all know that Democrats despise guns. *"Alright, not so fast,"* you're saying. We're already getting off on the wrong foot. Let me clarify. Typically, Democrats don't like guns that aren't theirs. Still too strong? How about this? Can we agree that it is very hard to find a Democrat with a "no compromise" position when it comes to the 2nd Amendment? Go ahead, name one. They are all willing to compromise the 2nd Amendment to better position themselves politically. Gun-ownership is constantly defamed, ridiculed and used as an excuse for every deranged lunatic's actions. It's never the killer's fault, and always the gun's. It seems to be almost ingrained in our language to say things like, *"I support the 2nd Amendment but..."* Some think its ok to bend *the right to keep and bear* in a way that we don't see with any other Constitutionally recognized right. It also seems that our friends on the left are the ones pushing to make this type of behavior acceptable. Acceptable? Heck, they want it to be common practice. Nevermind that; they not only want to bend the 2nd Amendment, they want "gun/people control" to be mandatory. But you already knew

33

that so let me get to the point. The point is really a question that I constantly work on answering. How do they get that way?

Why is the left so galvanized on the gun issue and how does it happen? What happens to them that doesn't usually happen to conservative-minded people? Watching people on the left descend on causes touted by their party is like watching metal shavings cling to a magnet. If you manage to pull them off their position for a minute, they quickly snap back in place as soon as you let go. What drives them and how is it that they prevent themselves from looking at a topic from a different perspective?

I was outside a hotel lobby in Chicago waiting for my ride to the airport after a conference, talking with some folks who were staying at the hotel. A conversation started and because of my gold rifle pen clip in the chest pocket of my suit jacket, it quickly turned into a conversation about guns. One person in particular was very outspoken about guns and I knew it would be a struggle if I were to take him down the road of logic. Plus, I only had about ten minutes. This person was as far left on the gun spectrum as you could imagine but I was able to help him see a couple very important things that were missing from his evaluation process. I was able to bring him around to an understanding that a baseball bat is no match for a home-invader with a gun as much as he wanted to make it so in his mind. You see, he found every way possible to denounce gun ownership because he was committed to his position. I needed to help him see the simple physics of a baseball bat having a swing-radius of approximately 6 feet while a handgun can accurately project a chunk of lead from a distance of 25 yards or more.

Once he was able to honestly assess the difference in effectiveness between a Louisville Slugger and a handgun on a logical level he was telling me that he understood why some people would prefer a gun for home-defense. *"OK, great."* I was actually getting somewhere so I kept asking him to try and see other benefits of gun-ownership without falling back to the typical position of "guns only being used for killing." We talked about competitive shooting, hunting and the value of collectable firearms. We were actually getting somewhere. Well, until I used the term "2nd Amendment." Something happened to my anti-gun friend as soon as I said those words. He went sideways and referred back to his original stance of *"yeah but, no one needs an assault weapon,"* almost in a robotic way as his wife gently tugged on his shirt sleeve. It was like I let go of the metal shavings and they quickly clung back to the magnet. Something about the term "2nd Amendment" made me lose him.

I learned that the term "2nd Amendment" means something to people on the left, and it's not good. I understand terminology and I discuss the topic in great detail as it relates to the gun conversation. I know what a powerful tool it is in shaping the minds of people to gain their support on issues. I see how effective terminology is when companies use it to encourage us to give up our money for products and services, but this was different. The way this man reacted was not typical of what I usually see. He appeared to have a physical reaction when I said "2nd Amendment." I could hear the anger in his voice as he took a much more aggressive approach to the conversation. Something happened to him. He had a Mr. Hyde moment and it resonated. I could feel it. The term "2nd Amendment" made him mad. When gun-owners talk about the 2nd Amendment, it comes with a sense of ownership and pride; something of value that deserves to be cherished and protected. When an Anti-Gunner hears the term "2nd Amendment," they qualify it as some type of radical right-wing battle-cry. The term "2nd Amendment" is their kryptonite.

Somehow they have been taught to hate it as if it was an assault on their values.

I've learned that the 2nd Amendment is an obstacle to Anti-Gunners. It's not something they respect or appreciate as much as they argue to the contrary. Many on the left have been conditioned to associate the 2nd Amendment (and gun-ownership in general) with anger and they often see it as a political threat. To some, the "2nd Amendment" are fighting words because they know it is the only thing standing in the way of their government controlled, structured, Utopian society. In other words, their bubble. They want their Utopian fantasy but *"those damn gun-owners won't give up their freedom or their guns."* I'll get more into this later. Don't let me forget. But for now, let's talk about how and why they so easily fall in line when it comes to defending the idea of unarmed helplessness.

We see unification among Democrats on many different political issues but we don't always understand how they can so easily conform to whatever agenda issues are put forth by their party. You've seen the rallies. They are usually large anger-filled gatherings that start off with the *appearance* of fighting for justice and quickly turn into irrational hate parties that accomplish nothing but destruction and division. They know it and the rest of America knows it as well, but it doesn't stop them from gravitating toward each other in a mission to punish and destroy their opposition. When their opposition doesn't exist, they create one. The most recent targets have been "racists," "Nazis" and "toxic masculinity." None of which seem to exist in numbers anywhere near what the justice-warriors claim or would like there to be so they have to perpetuate the narrative that these things are running rampant. When was the last time you actually saw a "Nazi" and how many "racists" do you know? The idea that now all of a sudden, men have "toxic masculinity" is the newest and least credible claim yet, but it doesn't matter, because ridding the world of theses "problems" is not the Social Justice Warrior's end goal. You see, along with creating an imaginary opposition, the radical left is able to simultaneously create a "popular table" at which they can claim domain. They need a bad guy so they can position themselves as the good guys and receive praise at the "popular table."

Once the political popular table is established, those who need validation will quickly rush to get a seat. They will often abandon their own personal values and beliefs for the reassurance and acceptance of their peers. I talk more about the popular table in "Good Gun Bad Guy - Behind the Lies of the Anti-Gun Radical" but for quick reference, refer to any middle school cafeteria and I am sure you will find a popular table. Those who host the "popular table" provide a value to those who need to be part of the winning team. The "popular table" always projects the perception that they are winning, whether accurate or not. The Democratic party also projects the perception that they are winning, whether accurate or not. It doesn't matter as much if they are actually winning, as long as their popular table occupants *believe* they are winning.

Committing to uphold the anti-gun doctrine often starts as an inquisitive topic for most people; something they typically don't know much about but understand it is a topic that has become divisive by nature. As long as the messaging is consistent and the person has limited firearms knowledge they can be encouraged to embrace an anti-gun stance. You see, people who are educated on firearms are not typically good recruits because they can't be easily manipulated to fear guns but people with limited knowledge to begin with can be "informed" in ways that guide their thought-process and shape their belief structure. This is not exclusive to the gun conversation, as I am sure you can imagine. We see this everywhere.

If we continue to use the hypothetical "popular table" for a minute, we can imagine the conversations that take place about guns. Most of us don't have to imagine these conversations because we have heard them first hand. I found myself part of the anti-gun crowd for short period of my life and I remember how the people whom I trusted, tried getting me on board by using "scare-tactics." I know the encouragement used to recruit people and I understand the leverage used to retain their loyalty. It's ugly and the people who host the popular table will use any manipulative strategy possible to keep their subjects dependent on their support. This strategy is also used when locking families into the welfare system. Teach a man to fish and he will be self-sufficient. Keep giving him fish and you own him. Keep giving insecure people the false sense of esteem and they become drunk on it while never learning how to build it themselves.

The anti-gun position quickly becomes a personal issue for some when they recognize their peers and family members supporting gun control, restrictions, and other components within the anti-gun sphere of interests. It becomes personal because they make it personal and when the facts don't line up with their position they justify their position by using the new term "my truth." Somehow leftists have found a new way to push their fantasies on you by re-defining "their wishes" as "their truth" and somehow it magically gives credibility to their argument. Regardless of fact-based truth, the new anti-gun recruits are fueled by and locked in to their mission to disarm the population. Once we make something personal, it is very difficult to look at it objectively and Anti-Gunners quickly make the gun debate personal. Personal ownership of the anti-gun position is the strongest tool in the Anti-2nd Amendment

Radical's tool box. They get people to own their anti-gun position by getting them to spread the word and take a position of justice warrior through their activism. Get it? Once you claim a team, your team is the best. You buy the Seahawks hat, jersey and mousepad. Now you're a Seattle Seahawks fan and nothing anyone can say will change that.

> *"Save lives not guns."*
> *"How many babies have to die?"*
> *"Ban assault weapons."*
> *"Never again."*
> *"Blood on your hands."*
> *"Stop the NRA."*

...and the list of personal commitment and enrollment into the anti-gun club goes on and on. Once a person paints one of these slogans on a sign and marches through the streets in front of national tv cameras, they are committed to the cause. Think about that. You've seen the protesters. You've seen how invested they are. You can imagine the level of gun-fear they have cultivated in their minds and you can almost feel the level of hatred they have developed toward you, the law-abiding gun owner. Do you honestly think turning back is an easy thing for them to do? Do you really think that FBI statistics are going to help them see their ignorance and switch sides? This isn't about statistics. This isn't even about saving lives. This is about indoctrination and leverage over the minds of people who can no longer critically think for themselves. They certainly can't look at the topic of guns with any clarity.

A genuine fear of guns starts to develop the longer a person is influenced by the anti-gun crowd. Regardless of personal belief and experience, Anti-Gunners typically find ways within their own thought-process to justify gun-hate and go along with the mission of their anti-gun peers. Even as they continue to see millions of Americans disregard their illogical, fact-less anti-gun position, they do not waiver. Their "my truth" personal ownership of the cause trumps all sense of reason and reality. A few can be helped but most cannot.

One thing Anti-Gunners do to solidify the notion in their own minds that guns don't belong in society is hold "gun buy backs." Gun buy-back programs have been a dismal failure for anti-gun groups in America. The radical-left praises their Australian counterparts for the "brave" work they did to control gun-ownership down under, but in America, gun-grabbers are not met with the same enthusiasm. In Australia, the "gun buy-back" was mandatory. Gun-hating leftists know that mandatory gun buy-backs are not possible in America, so they simulate the process. Don't think for a minute that they don't salivate over this type of event. They want to see gun-owners admit defeat and cower at the feet of the socialist gun-grabbers as they turn in their guns. American buy-backs are a way for the Anti-2nd Amendment Radicals to feel like they have won something. It's like receiving a trophy for coming in last.

With Police Officers on hand to take the guns into custody, the gun-grabbers hand out a measly compensation. Groups have tried to offer money for guns in an attempt to (as they claim) *"get those dangerous guns off the streets,"* but have failed in accomplishing any real results. What typically happens is those who already fear guns and hate the idea of gun-ownership will show up with some non-functioning relic that has been collecting rust in the basement, to exchange it for fifty dollars. They leave feeling like they have done their part in saving the world and the money is gone that afternoon after a trip to Chipotle. Or worse, as has happened several times - Nana brings in those old things Grandpa had in the attic since he got home in '46 ...and another valuable piece of American history is destroyed in the name of liberal-ideology or insanity.

Occasionally, gun-owners will exchange junk and use the "buy-back" money to invest in newer firearms or more ammo. If only the Anti-2nd Amendment Radicals knew about this.

I always questioned the motive of the "buy-backers" because their method spoke louder than their results. What I mean is, the media hype always presented these "buy-backs" as a huge event that would really make a difference in solving the problem of their so called "gun-violence," while producing next to zero attendance. I'll get into the "gun-violence" lie later. So why do they really do "gun buy-backs?" Well, we know it's not to take guns off the streets because time after time they have failed. This was clearly seen in Saratoga Springs, NY when Mayor Meg Kelly hosted a gun buy-back only to produce laughable results.

"We believe that if people are given a safe way to deposit their firearms, they don't mind. It'll help all citizens in our area. It might prevent needless accidents, injuries and tragedies," said Mayor Kelly.

"Fewer guns in our city equates to less chance of accidents or impulsive violence resulting from their easy access," said Courtney DeLeonardis, who is the chair of the Saratoga Springs Democratic Committee, which supports the effort. "When people see that others care enough about this danger to organize an event like this, we hope many may be prompted to bring in unwanted firearms."

Although the Democrat backed, self-indulgent, feel-good party in Saratoga Springs pulled in a measly 60 firearms from attics across the city in exchange for $100 gift cards, I stopped laughing when I noticed the real motive behind the sham. In the two quotes above are some very revealing statements of how Anti-2nd Amendment Radicals really think.

When Mayor Kelly stated in Saratoga Living Newspaper that *"We believe,"* what she must have meant was, a small group of Anti-Gun Democrats on the City Council Board "believe" and everyone else should get on board or you will be part of the minority. But you are supposed to think that this is a majority of the community and if you disagree, you are of the minority. This is a typical left-wing "popular table" strategy. Other key words she used were *"safe"* and *"they don't mind,"* further encouraging the notion that this is what people want. Remember, out of the Saratoga Springs population of almost 28,000, in a State with a population of nearly 20,000,000, only 60 dusty old guns were sold in exchange for $100 gift cards. Hardly a popular event but perception is the goal here. Don't take your eye off the ball like they want you to.

Both Mayor Kelly and Democratic Committee Member Courtney DeLeonardis both referenced *"accidents"* as being part of their motivation. This is part of the infamous "Toddler and the Gun" fear campaign that Anti-Gunners and Radicals often use. The idea here is to make you think that cute little diaper-bottomed babies across the country are constantly getting ahold of their parents guns that are irresponsibly left loaded and lying around the house. The truth is, this almost never happens and more children die by being accidentally run over in their own driveway than ever do from any type of accidental firearm discharge. It's curious how the gun-grabbers never want to talk about child driveway deaths. It makes you think they don't really care about saving lives. There have never been any documented firearm "accidents" in Saratoga Springs that I could find so I never quite understand how the gun-grabbers justify this type of rhetoric in their minds. You'd think if they really wanted to save lives they would focus on an area where they could actually have an impact. The truth is, most Anti-2nd Amendment Radicals don't really want to save lives as much as they want to ban guns. More on that later.

Another interesting quote from our gun-grabbing friend Courtney DeLeonardis was her *"impulsive violence resulting from their easy access"* comment. When you get into the thought-process of the Anti-Gunner, you start to see that they really do believe that guns *cause* people to do bad things. They will typically take the responsibility *off* the human and place it on the gun. I know it's hard to grasp the notion that people cannot recognize the *person* being the culprit but they seem to discard the idea of free-will when it comes to the topic of guns. There are people who truly believe that when a gun is present, some people will be compelled to act violently. In other words, if it wasn't for the gun, the person would have been friendly or maybe even shared their sandwich with you. But because the gun was there, they somehow turn into a violent monster. What does that say about the person who believes this?

Think about this for a minute; wouldn't the person who claims guns *cause* violent behavior, have to believe that *they* too might react similarly in the presence of a gun? Otherwise, how could they project that "reactive-violence" thought-process onto others if they didn't first think it in their own mind? Are they mind-readers or do they believe the thoughts occurring in their head is what others are thinking too? This type of thinking is childish and should make everyone wonder who the real dangerous people are in our society; the law-abiding gun-owners or those who, (in their own minds) imagine guns causing impulsive violence?

So, what is the real motive behind gun buy-backs? Why do I call it a "sham?" Why do I suggest it's not really about "taking guns off the streets" or "keeping people safe?" Let me give you another example and see if I can do a good job of helping you connect the dots.

In Hempstead, NY, local officials hosted a new and unique type of "gun buy-back" during the Christmas holiday of 2018 that is reported to have begun in 2015. Hempstead officials believe that it is important to take those "dangerous" toy guns out of the hands of children so they rallied a bunch of 4 year-olds and explained to them just how bad guns are. The kiddos were also taught that even the plastic Nerf gun that Santa brought them should be turned in because, well… just because. Obviously, Santa must be one of those deplorable, gun-toting conservatives and even he must be taught the ways of the new Leftist World Order. You're not going to like this but if you decide to read on, don't hate me.

Hempstead Village Trustee LaMont Jackson told WABC-TV that Hempstead officials don't want children "playing with guns." - The Blaze

"The purpose is to offer safe alternatives to toy guns," Jackson explained. "We don't want the kids playing with guns. Guns are dangerous."

"Saying no to guns is important. Even toy guns," said Mayor Don Ryan.

Hempstead Village Police Department Lt. Derek Warner told WABC-TV that parents could be putting their kids lives at risk by gifting them toy guns for the holidays. "Toy guns can be a dangerous item to give your children."

Sean Acosta, a former New York Police Department Officer reportedly told children earlier in December that he wants "to make sure when you grow up, nothing happens to you."

So here we have the Mayor, Police Department and Village Trustee of Wackytown, all trying desperately to encourage kids to fear guns and convince them that even toy guns are dangerous. Never-mind putting together firearm safety classes and help children gain a healthy understanding of guns. Never-mind teaching kids to respect guns and use them properly and safely as they grow up. Never-mind teaching kids about the Bill of Rights and how the 2nd Amendment was written to remind Government who they work for. Oh no. That's crazy talk.

"Let's indoctrinate them early on and build in them, a healthy fear so they never want to own a gun and demonize those who do."

Here's the irony and here is also where the Hempstead hired employees get sinister. As it turns out, attendance to the Hempstead Child Toy Gun Buy-Back was not what officials had hoped for. Some kids showed up but they weren't carrying Super-Soakers or suction cup revolvers. Nope, most came empty-handed. So what would a good group of Anti-2nd Amendment Radicals do? You guessed it. They lined the kids up and provided them with toy guns so they could wait in line to turn them in. Just like in a real communist country.

Go ahead, read that again if you have to. Yes, they provided the toy guns to those children who didn't have any so they could wait in line to turn them in. This is not about keeping children safe. It's about training them to be "anti-gun."

Apparently this group of city officials felt the need to manufacture a toy gun buy-back and force little children to participate in their insanity. Why would they do this, you might ask? Probably for the same ideological reason a parent would dress their eleven year old boy in drag and put him on stage so grown men could throw dollar bills at him. Yes, that happened too, but let's go back and revisit the "adult buy-backs" for a better understanding of how gun buy-backs relate to anti-gun indoctrination. We know the buy-backs are unsuccessful but the Gun-Grabbers continue to facilitate them. Why? Do they just like the authoritarian act of taking guns? Maybe. Do they actually believe that they are removing a significant number of guns from the streets? Only if they are brain dead and can't see their own results, so... maybe. Do they truly believe that they are "making people safer?" Doubt it. Do they want to get people comfortable with the idea of gun buy-backs? I think we're getting closer. Do they want people to see *other people* turning in guns and think, *"if all these people are giving up their guns, maybe it's not such a bad idea?"* Now we're get warmer.

So what happens when adults don't seem to be interested in buy-backs or don't want to play along in the numbers these American Communists would like? Is it possible that the gun-grabbers may be looking to the next generation of people who could potentially vote for anti-gun politicians? I think we're right over the target. Now think about what must be going on in the minds of the people putting this child gun buy-back fiasco together.

"Well Don, we don't have many kids and the ones that are here don't have any toy guns. What should we do?"

"Go buy them some toy guns and line them up so they can wait in line to trade them in for other safer toys. The idea here is to make them go through the motions. We just want them to understand that guns are bad and to help them feel comfortable with mandatory government control. That's all. Just condition them." – These are not real quotes. The photo below however, is real.

Image source: WABC-TV video screenshot

The despicable "toy gun buy-back" is one of many ways our young people are being exposed to the anti-gun message. It's part of a larger narrative and fear-campaign that is designed to help people fear guns and hate those who support gun-ownership. I never said you would like what you read here, but

I can promise you, that when you close this book, you will do it with a much better understanding of the Anti-2nd Amendment Radical's strategy to disarm America. I will also promise you that you will be much better equipped to defend that precious 2nd Amendment after our 250 page conversation.

2. RIGHTS VS. PRIVILEGES

To get people to conform to government rule, you must condition them to view rights as privileges.

Have you ever heard someone say, *"I support the 2nd Amendment but I think we need "Common Sense Gun-Restrictions?"*

Well, you can't do both. You can't support my right to keep and bear arms while restricting my right to keep and bear arms. It just doesn't work like that. And the term "common sense," That's just something they add to try and make you look irrational if you don't go along with them... because who wouldn't want to have common sense? The truth is, there is nothing that the Anti-Gun Radicals propose that has any common sense.

But let's talk about how they define a "right." They clearly get "privilege" and "right" mixed up. The Anti-Gunners can't seem to decipher the difference. A "privilege" is something that is given by man and can be taken away by man. We use privileges when we discipline our kids. *"If you don't finish your dinner, you lose the privilege of staying up past 10pm."* Privileges are sometimes used to gain leverage. *"If you don't do what I want, I may take away privileges."* Privileges can only exist if one person (or group of people) has the power to authorize the privilege and another person (or group of people) is the recipient of the privilege. A privilege can also be something that becomes accessible if certain criteria are met. If you

49

become a member to a social club, your membership dues may afford you privileges that are inaccessible to others.

"Rights" however, are not given by man. That's what makes them different. A "right" is a moral entitlement, inherent at birth. God-given. Rights are part of our humanity and in America, we recognize the rights of all law-abiding citizens in a little document called "The Bill of Rights." But rights can be kinda' greasy for the gun-grabbers because they can't quite get a grip on controlling your rights. Privileges are much easier to control, so they need to convolute the definitions of the two.

Anti-Gunners seem to be unable to understand the concept that certain things can't be controlled. In America (the land of the free), socialist-minded people are driven crazy by this concept. This is why they create things like "political correctness." Political correctness is their creative and desperate way of controlling the right of people to speak freely. So, you have the right to free-speech, but political correctness controls the parameters of that speech without using legislation. And by the way, it infuriates them when people pay no attention to their social rules.

A dead give away to how Anti-Gunners and some of the socialist-minded ideology think about rights, is when they say things like, *"Don't worry, we're not going to take away your guns. Your rights are guaranteed."* They imply that they *can* take away your rights by saying they're not going to. The implication here is very important because the fear of losing rights puts gun-owners in a defensive position and the gun-grabbers know this. Let's think about that for a minute. Are rights guaranteed? No they're not. Does someone give you your rights? No. So who is guaranteeing them? You can't give someone rights, and you can't guarantee someone's rights. If you could, they wouldn't be called rights. They would be called privileges. Rights are not guaranteed. Rights can only be honored or violated. This is why we must sometimes fight to protect our rights from enemies who want to violate them. In other words "rights" must sometimes be defended whether we like it or not.

To an Anti-2nd Amendment Radical, your rights just get in the way of their control, and they hate that because they can't do anything about it. As the progressive indoctrination continues to grind it's way through our society, people are slowly being trained to view "rights" as "privileges." That's why some people think it's possible to support our 2nd Amendment right, while simultaneously implementing restrictions on it. To them, it makes perfect sense because they live by government enforced rules, regulations and restrictions. They see nothing wrong with this. That's the scary part.

We can argue with them about gun-statistics all day long, but until we get into the mud with them on the way they are being taught to think, we won't get anywhere. We never talk about the disorientated and manipulated thought process of the Anti-Gunners. ...and we should be talking about that, a lot. That is the real problem. That thought-process is what encourages violence and makes good people vulnerable. Their lack of understanding and their support for gun-restrictions that make good people vulnerable encourages violent behavior from criminals because the criminals know they have no opposition once their potential victims are disarmed. In their attempt to defeat their fellow American citizens in the gun-debate, the left becomes a friend to the criminals.

People on the political left are taught to confuse the definitions of rights and privileges only when it suits the agenda. They often recognize the right of free speech because it's not something that they would ever want to lose for themselves, but they also don't want anyone with opposing views to have that same right. So what would they do in such a difficult position? They create "political correctness." Political correctness is simply a way of shaming those, with opposing views, into keeping quiet. They are able to do this without implementing legislation. They're not stupid. Why in the world would they want to create laws that would affect them negatively? The key word is control.

Sometimes radical views go so far that some people truly do lose sight of the fact that we all have rights in America. This typically happens with people on the left because they consistently live in a bubble where the only thought process they are exposed to, is that of which, views the Constitution as an irrelevant, outdated document. A perfect example of this was an interview with the infamous Christiane Amanpour from CNN. Christiane interviewed James Comey in early April 2019 and when referring to the speech of Donald Trump supporters that she didn't like, she said the following:

"Of course 'lock her up' was a feature of the 2016 Trump campaign. Do you in retrospect, wish that people like yourself, the head of the FBI, I mean the people in charge of law and order, had shut down that language? That it was dangerous potentially. That it could've created violence. That it's kind of hate speech. Should that have been allowed?"

Yes, she really said this. The scary part is that, given the ability, people like Christiane *would* shut down opposing views. This is clearly a woman who has lost sight of the Bill of Rights, and she exposed herself on national television. This example of the left-wing thought process reflects the entire ideology and the desire to implement as many control strategies as possible upon people. Christiane gave us a great insight into just how badly some people wish to control their opposition with punishment by law-enforcement.

Another way those on the political left use rights and privileges to their advantage is within the abortion conversation. You'll notice how they are quick to view the 2nd Amendment as a government issued privilege that can be restricted and regulated, but when it comes to abortion, they see it quite differently. They'll say things like *"we need common sense gun-control,"* but ending a life in the womb, somehow becomes *"a woman's 'right' to choose."* The truth is, one is actually a "right" and one is a government issued "privilege." They just conveniently get the two mixed up. It must be complicated for them to keep all their rules straight. Can you imagine navigating through life with such a complex and inconsistent set of conflicting ideas and social rules?

This Anti-Gun mindset brings with it a lot of ridiculous catch-phrases and one-liners designed to position gun-ownership as a privilege rather than a right.

Don't you love it when an Anti-Gunner says, *"Why does anybody need an AR 15?"* How about the question: *"Why do you need to carry a gun, what are you so afraid of?"* Sure we have our bumber-sticker responses too, like, *"It's not the Bill of Needs,"* and *"My rights don't end where your feeling begin,"* but the truth is, we usually find ourselves trying to justify our gun-ownership to some Knucklehead who has never even held a gun in their hand.

You see, Anti-Gunners look at gun ownership as something that is done out of fearful-need. If you understand their perspective and limited knowledge on the topic, it's really no surprise that they can't comprehend gun-ownership in a logical way. The entire topic is purely emotionally-driven for them. They think the only reason you would have a gun is because you *need* it. Why do they think that? Because that's the only reason they can imagine *themselves* having a gun.

When an Anti-Gunner asks you the question, *"Why do you need a gun?"* They're not asking you because they really want to know. They're asking because they know you're going to have a hard time answering the question. They believe, the only reason to have a gun is that you need one and they don't look at the gun conversation from a perspective of rights, self-defense or personal responsibility. They look at gun ownership through a lens of fear. Anti-Gunners typically approach the gun conversation from a scared, fearful perspective. Remember, they only view guns as devices designed specifically to kill people. Sure, they may say that they understand the concept of hunting and sport shooting but when you bring up the conversation of guns the Anti-Gunner will typically speak on the topic while envisioning murder and mayhem. That's how they've been trained. So because they are conditioned to see gun ownership as a way for people to kill, and because they shut out all information to the contrary, it's difficult for them to comprehend owning guns for any positive reason.

When an Anti-Gunner asks you why you need a gun, they want and expect to hear you say you own a gun because you're scared. They hope to make you look irrational as they laugh in disbelief. But the truth is, gun owners aren't scared at all. Gun owners will typically own guns out of a sense of personal responsibility; the responsibility to protect themselves, their families and the good people around them. Fear is not usually a component for gun-owners. If fear is initially a reason for gun-ownership, it usually doesn't last long because after a new gun owner becomes familiar and confident with their guns and the idea of gun ownership, the fear goes away and the gun serves a new purpose. It's frustrating to watch gun-owners bend over backwards to justify their gun ownership to these condescending Anti-Gunners. If we can recognize the illogical perspective of the gun-fear crowd, we have a chance at helping them see their own ignorance.

Because gun owners don't look at guns through a lens of fearful need (rather a lens of responsibility) they often have a hard time answering the question, *"Why do you need a gun?"* "Need" is often a strange concept for gun owners, but it's the most obvious reason for the uninformed Anti-Gunner. So any time an Anti-Gunner asks you why you need a gun, remember they're asking because they think you think like them and they want the opportunity to make you look fearful and irrational. It's a gotcha question. Don't fall for it.

Left wing Anti-Gunners have been trained and conditioned to fear guns more than any other dangers in our society. They're taught that guns are the problem, that guns are the cause of violence, and that guns are the scariest thing in the world. Once the Anti-2nd Amendment Radicals are able to cripple the emotionally-reactive Anti-Gunners with fear, they capitalize on it. By using the fear of guns that they create, they can then rally those who fear guns to their anti-gun cause. The math is really very simple; Create fear, blame guns for that fear, pretend that a small radical group of gun owners are putting everyone in danger, propose a solution to relieve that fear in the hearts of people. You guessed it, the solution is of course to get rid of the guns. Those who have been terrorized are sure to go along and vote for more gun-restrictions. The gun-grabbers know exactly what they are doing.

"We cannot let a minority of people — and that's what it is, it is a minority of people — hold a viewpoint that terrorizes the majority of people." – Hillary Clinton

---

Along with being terrorized by anti-gun gun propaganda, the emotionally-weak voters are taught that criminals, thugs and terrorists are just victims of society. So their fear of guns becomes much stronger than their fear of criminals. That leads them to the only explanation for owning a gun, in their mind, being a very intense and desperate "need." Otherwise, why would you do it? And in most cases, because they are taught to have compassion for killers, they don't see a "need" for anyone to carry a gun.

The Anti-Gun Radical's fear of guns is much stronger than their fear of criminals.

Anti-Gunners are more scared of guns than they are of thugs, terrorists and killers because that's the way they've been taught. That's the way they are programmed and conditioned on a daily basis through media, movies and public schools. So imagine for a minute, a person with very specific societal beliefs. Let's call her Miss Ledd. We know this person is not real, but play along. Our imaginary friend Miss Ledd holds the following beliefs:

- Miss Ledd believes that guns are the *cause* of human violence.
- Miss Ledd believes that guns *make* people to do bad things.
- Miss Ledd believes that guns are dangerous and unpredictable.
- Miss Ledd believes that if killers didn't have access to guns, they wouldn't kill.

- Miss Ledd believes that gun restrictions prevent the bad guys from getting guns.

Now also imagine,

- Miss Ledd believes that radical Islamic terrorists are victims of religious bigotry.
- Miss Ledd believes gang members are victims of an unjust society.
- Miss Ledd believes that all who enter America illegally are innocent mothers and children seeking asylum.
- Miss Ledd believes that radical politically-motivated groups like Antifa are trying to stop hate and violence.

Now I know the media and left-wing politicians would never convince people to think like this, but if they did, would it be any wonder why these people can't see the topic of guns with logic? Would it be surprising that liberal-progressives could support open borders and radical Islam while simultaneously supporting the disarming of their own fellow American citizens? How does this make any sense? I'm sure you've asked the same question and I've discussed it before, but let's take it from a slightly different perspective.

Anti-Gunners see guns and gun ownership through a lens of fear and irrational need. Gun-owners see gun ownership through a lens of responsibility. Sure, initially when we start carrying a gun we might do it out of a sense of need but that need quickly turns into responsibility as we start to be comfortable with firearms and start to understand them. The thing that Anti-Gunners will never understand is that, aside from hunting, sporting and collecting; gun-owners own guns out of a responsibility to keep themselves, their families and the good people around them safe, not out of a sense of irrational fear like Anti-Gunners might think. Anti-Gunners will never let themselves get that far because the minute they attempt to gain knowledge on the topic of guns, they are shunned by their peers. If they go against the anti-gun doctrine they will be considered a traitor to the gun-control cause. They'll get kicked off the popular table. If, on the rare occasion, an Anti-Gunner breaks away from the progressive social parameters and actually goes to the range, the event *can* have a positive affect. They may actually have a good time. Depending on how indoctrinated they have been to that point, will determine if their appreciation for guns will last.

Sure they have been told countless times that the 2nd Amendment is a right but they don't want it to be. They want it to be a government issued privilege. This is why you'll hear Anti-Gunners say things like, *"I support your second amendment but I think we need common-sense gun restrictions."* They use the term "common-sense" because they want to be perceived as the ones with common sense, even though the policies they support are often the cause of massive loss of life. They will often use the word "your" when referring to the 2nd Amendment because it is a way for them to psychologically disassociate themselves with anything related to gun-ownership. This is a way to keep them in the clear and avoid any association.

Remember, if they take ownership, they would be compelled to defend it. So it is "your" 2nd Amendment. They will condescend you and insult your intelligence by saying they support "your" rights while simultaneously trying to undermine those very rights. They actually believe that they can guilt you into going along with their dangerous policies by making you fear being seen as having "no sense," hence the "common sense" gun-restrictions. They have been and continue to be conditioned to blur the definitions of rights and privileges.

They don't see the difference. They are also taught to fight their battle against gun-ownership because they believe the "cause" is the most important thing and they have a duty to make a change in the world. In reality, they have lost sight of the most important, underlying, American value - freedom.

Ben D. Bunked: Nobody needs an AR15.

C. Clearly: Well ok, but what do you mean by *need*?

Ben D. Bunked: You know, nobody should have them. They're unnecessary. Nobody needs to have one.

C. Clearly: So if nobody *needs* to have one, they shouldn't have one?

Ben D. Bunked: That's right. They're only designed for killing mass amounts of people. If we want the mass carnage to stop, we should take these deadly killing devices away from people. Ban 'em.

C. Clearly: Well nobody needs to smoke cigarettes, but I don't hear you talking about the 480,000 cigarette related deaths per year, or the tens-of-thousands of auto-related deaths each year. Do you also want to ban cigarettes and cars or are you only concerned with deaths when a gun is involved?

Ben D. Bunked: That's irrelevant. I'm focused on these dangerous assault weapons.

C. Clearly: Well, that's painfully obvious. Ok. So if what you say is true, that nobody *needs* an AR15, therefore nobody should have one, what guns *do* people need?

Ben D. Bunked: Well,... I don't know, a hunting rifle.

C. Clearly: So, should people be allowed to have a hunting rifle because they *need* it?

Ben D. Bunked: Sure. Whatever.

C. Clearly: The reason I'm asking is because if you are arguing for the banning of AR15's from a measurement of need, that kinda presupposes that you think some guns *are* needed. What other guns *do* people need if they don't need an AR15?

Ben D. Bunked: Damn it, people don't need guns at all! Any of them!

C. Clearly: Ok. At least now you're letting me know how you *really* feel. So is it safe to say that when you tell me AR15's should be banned because nobody *needs* them, you are really just using that as an excuse? You really don't want anyone to have guns at all.

Ben D. Bunked: Yes. You damn gun-owners put everyone in danger and if I had my way none of you would have guns because you don't need any of them!!!

[long pause]

C. Clearly: Let me ask you another question.

Ben D. Bunked: Fine.

C. Clearly: What if gun-ownership is not about *need* at all?

Ben D. Bunked: What do you mean?

C. Clearly: What if gun-ownership is about something else, a responsibility for safety or just the freedom of recreation, but you've been convinced that your best argument against guns is to argue the "need" aspect?

Ben D. Bunked: I know, I know, now you're gonna tell me it's a right.

C. Clearly: Yes… it is… but you don't want it to be. Correct? [pause] It's ok, be honest. People have a right that you don't like because it scares you. Or it pisses you off. Or both.

Ben D. Bunked: Fine. I'll be honest. Guns *do* scare me because they're unpredictable and extremely dangerous. And you f***ing gun-owners don't give a s**t!

C. Clearly: OK. You are obviously upset. Why? We are just having a conversation and now you are taking it to a new level. What are you most angry at right now?

Ben D. Bunked: I'm not just angry. I'm furious because you people are so stubborn and you won't compromise.

C. Clearly: Compromise on what?

Ben D. Bunked: On your damn guns. They are so important to you that you would rather have people die in the streets for your own selfishness.

C. Clearly: Well, that's not true, but what if this isn't about guns at all? What if this is about the ability of everyone, including you, to be able to protect themselves and their families? What if we see your rights as a higher value than you do? What if we see your rights as more important for future generations than

61

you see them because you have been convinced that people are "dying in the streets?" What if we understand that the number of deaths would be far greater if good people were subjected to the restrictions you are trying to put on them? What if you are clouded by images of death and destruction and can't see the eventual outcome of the loss of your own rights?

Ben D. Bunked: I don't care about your damn rights! These guns are deadly!

C. Clearly: Ah. There you go. So what's really making you so angry?

Ben D. Bunked: Talking to you people is like trying to break through a brick wall.

C. Clearly: So the conversation with me is making you angry?

Ben D. Bunked: Yes because you won't compromise. I mean, you won't see it any other way. I mean...

C. Clearly: Finally, the truth comes out. You're angry because you can't win the debate. Are you sure, you're not the one who is unable to see this any other way?

Ben D. Bunked: Absolutely not!

C. Clearly: Hold on a minute. You used the word "compromise." You also implied that you're angry because I won't see it your way. But let me ask you about compromise. Which of *your* values would you be willing to compromise?

[pause]

Ben D. Bunked: What do you mean?

C. Clearly: Well, you said we won't compromise. It implies that *you* would. You do know that self-preservation and protecting the lives around us is a value to gun-owners right?

Ben D. Bunked: Well, Sure. Whatever.

C. Clearly: Name something that's a high value to you.

Ben D. Bunked: What do you mean?

C. Clearly: Tell me something that is important to you, something that you value.

Ben D. Bunked: Making change in the world.

C. Clearly: Why is "making change in the world" so important to you?

Ben D. Bunked: That's a stupid question.

C. Clearly: Ok. Humor me.

Ben D. Bunked: Because if I make change in the world my actions are worthwhile.

C. Clearly: So, you need to be effective?

Ben D. Bunked: Yes. Exactly. I need to be effective.

C. Clearly: Do you see the difference between my argument and yours?

Ben D. Bunked: What?

C. Clearly: Your ultimate goal may be to save lives but your actions are focused on the cause (or the fight) rather than the ultimate value. You Anti-Gunners seem to be so focused on having your personal actions be effective, or winning the debate, or making your point that you lose sight of the real goal. "Saving lives." We gun-owners have never lost sight of that.

Ben D. Bunked: What do you mean?

C. Clearly: What I mean is, your fight "making change in the world" is a "cause." Our fight to ultimately save lives supports an inherent "value." The value of life. What you call a value, "making change in the world" or being "effective" is really about you. In other words, if you win the argument or shut me down, you feel successful. We gun-owners can win the argument and realize that we have done nothing to save lives. Just "winning the fight" doesn't satisfy us. We want to see that lives are saved and we want to make sure our families are protected.

Ben D. Bunked: But we too want to save lives.

C. Clearly: Maybe you do, but your fight has been so corrupted and you have become so obsessed with winning and defeating your opponent (me) that you lose sight of the real value. If you were able to put aside your personal need to win the argument and start focusing on saving lives, you and I could look at statistics from a non-biased perspective. We could ask people who have been in dangerous situations, how they would have felt if someone were there to protect them with a gun. We could get to the facts of how guns actually save millions of lives every year. But instead, we are arguing politics because you need to win the argument in order to "feel effective."

Ben D. Bunked: Well, I don't know...

C. Clearly: Let me bring you back to something you said a minute ago. You said we won't compromise and that talking with me is like trying to break through a brick wall.

Ben D. Bunked: Yes. It is.

C. Clearly: What if you have created the very brick wall you are trying to break through because you lost sight of the real value and you are hung up on winning a debate or shutting me down? Don't forget the value we gun-owners are defending.

Ben D. Bunked: You mean, saving lives?

C. Clearly: Yup. And what if we gun-owners aren't really the "shoot-em-up-recloses," you have been taught to believe? What if we have never lost sight of the *real* value and we have always been trying to help Anti-Gunners see that they have been taken down the path of fighting for a "cause" (winning an argument for political purposes) that's based on information that just isn't true. What if we watch you everyday as you desperately try to win the argument and we sit back and wonder how it's possible that you have become so consumed with perpetuating a fake gun narrative.

Ben D. Bunked: What information is fake?!

C. Clearly: For starters, your impression of gun-owners may not actually be what you have been consistently taught to believe and the idea that gun-free-zones make people safer is a lie. The semi-automatic verses automatic debate, the babies getting ahold of loaded guns, the gun-show loophole... the list goes on and on. The entire anti-gun propaganda circus is laughable but we watch you, not only embrace it, but perpetuate it. What if that "wall" you are trying to break through is really just a metaphor for winning the argument and you are trying to do it with false information and unjust anger that has been perpetuated by people with political motives?

Ben D. Bunked: Well, I don't know, but...

C. Clearly: Look, the thing is, we are not willing to compromise our value of preserving life just to appease a political opponent and we see very clearly, the fact that anti-gun advocates are fighting a battle for the wrong reasons. So let me ask you again, because you expressed frustration that we won't compromise. Which of your values are you willing to compromise?

3. POLITICAL RELIGION

When God is removed from society, those who need guidance will gravitate toward the closet thing they can find.

Democrats in congress will use things that people love as leverage against them. Let's use the abortion issue for a minute. But first, a couple questions. In what universe would it be ok to kill an unborn baby? What species makes it common practice to kill their own?

If you were to land on Earth for the first time from some far-off galaxy and you learned that some of the planet's inhabitants killed their own offspring on a regular basis while simultaneously protecting murderers by giving them areas of sanctuary where they were exempt from consequence of their own heinous acts, you would think you have entered the Twilight Zone. When you were to find out that these same people fought to make their fellow citizens unarmed and helpless and were willing to give up their own freedom in the hopes of being controlled by a ruling class of dictators, you would get back into your spaceship and hit the gas.

In America, it's not only legal to kill babies, it's celebrated. As a matter of fact, on January 22nd, 2019 New York Governor Cuomo directed One World Trade Center and other landmarks to be lit in pink in celebration of the signing of the "Reproductive Health Act." Why was this so important to the Democrat Governor? It was important because the

67

Reproductive Health Act included a provision that would allow abortions right up until the time of birth at the discretion of the mother. This is viewed by the Democrat party as a victory in the movement of 4th wave Feminism, not only as a freedom for women to "choose" but also as a statement to let men know that they have no business telling a woman what she can do with her body, even if that man is the father of the child. This may appear to those who support it as a win for women's rights but acts purely as a divisive strategy to split men and women politically while giving women a false sense of empowerment. Remember, that empowerment can be taken away by those who give it and Democrat politician will never let their voters forget it.

The Media, at the direction of Democrats in congress will always remind Democrat voters that those evil Republicans are lurking right around the corner just waiting to overturn Roe v. Wade and unless they continue to vote Democrat, they will lose their "right" to kill their unborn babies which they have been conditioned to see as a triumph over "oppression." Again, this may seem insane to people who value life but don't forget, a lot of effort has gone into the brainwashing of people on this topic for several decades and the emotional leverage is consistently used against those who have taken the bait. Similar to the left's position on gun-restrictions, punishment and public shaming will be applied should the voter...er, I mean person stray from the agenda.

"I think [Kavanaugh] intends to overturn Roe v. Wade, or limit it." "It could happen overnight. I think [he'll take] any opportunity to vote against Roe in any form, whether it's narrowing it or overturning it. He literally believes he can rule outside of precedent."

– NY Senator Kirsten Gillibrand

"No woman should be told she can't make her own decisions about her body. If women's reproductive rights come under attack, I will be standing up for women."
— CA Senator Kamala Harris

"No woman can call herself free who does not control her own body."
— Margaret Sanger

"Women and our right to choose were going to be challenged with Ashcroft around. When Bush appointed Ashcroft, I went out and got me four abortions. I stocked up. The doctor was like, 'Listen, you're not pregnant.' I said, 'Hey, just shut up and do your job. I'm exercising my right while I can, dammit.'"

— Wanda Sykes, Yeah, I said it

Now think about the leverage being used here. Those who are in favor of this horrific law feel empowered because they are now told abortion is a "right." Remember the definition of a right? A right is God-given and inherent at birth. Many would argue that God would not want us killing our own children for any reason, let alone because the child would be an inconvenience and definitely not at the time of natural birth, but the conditioning by liberal-progressive politicians and media has been relentless in its pursuits to change the way people think about this topic. Once abortion is believed to be a "right," "women's choice" and/or "healthcare," politicians can use it as leverage to garner votes. The truth is, unlike the 2nd Amendment (which actually is a right), abortion is not. Abortion has become a government issued privilege and has nothing to do with "healthcare." As a matter of fact, abortion

69

puts the health of the mother *at risk*. But remember the slogan, "A woman's right to choose." Which Amendment was that in again?

After the Judge Kavanaugh nomination to the Supreme Court, the abortion fear-mongering was quite intense. The never-ending stream of articles from every left-wing internet rag was relentless in its pursuit to scare liberals into creating a political stir to ultimately garner more left-wing voter support. Remember, no one likes their "rights" taken away. The problem with the abortion argument, is that it is far from a "right." It is a government issued "privilege" masked as a "right." They will also continue to cultivate the minds of malleable liberals that think killing their own babies is empowering.

Here is a quote taken from "The Cut" during the 2018 midterm elections:

"Two out of three anti-abortion ballot measures passed. First, the bad news: Alabama voters approved a ballot measure that declared support for "the sanctity of unborn life and the rights of unborn children," and to "provide that the constitution of this state does not protect the right to abortion or require the funding of abortion."

The scary part here is that people have been convinced that it is "bad news" when the sanctity of life is protected. The sickness we see in the abortion argument as well as in the minds of those who want to make their fellow citizens unarmed and helpless is not a genetic sickness. It's not a contagious disease. It is a sickness and brainwashing that is taught and must be continually cultivated. It is manifested through politics for the purpose of gathering as many votes as possible. The good news is, that should the indoctrination of leftists stop for a generation or two, Americans will default back to a more traditional, family orientated, God-loving set of principles. Leftists know this and will do anything they can to prevent it from happening which is why constant awareness of liberal issues must always dominate the media. It all comes down to swaying people at the polls. Politicians will use whatever leverage they can create to gain power over those who ultimately put them in office. The denigration of God and the encouragement of Atheism assists politicians in the ability to gain leverage over the minds of people. This is the point when some will put their political affiliation over their religion. To some, politics *is* their religion.

"OK, so why all the abortion talk? I thought this was about guns." It is, but more importantly, it's about the politics behind guns. So how does this abortion-leverage relate to guns?

Think about how easy it is to get liberal-progressives on board with a cause if they think losing their rights are at stake. Don't forget "rights" to them are really government-issued privileges and the "rights" they want are those of the new progressive ideology. Leftists don't seem to mind the idea of being controlled by their government if the rules are to their liking, but they can't stand the idea of living in a traditional-American society shaped by Conservative-minded, freedom-loving people.

If Democrats can make real Americans fearful of losing the 2nd Amendment, the thought is that they can create leverage over them to get what they want politically. This is why Democrats will push for sanctuary cities and illegal immigration while simultaneously restricting law-abiding citizens of their right to keep and bear arms. It puts the law-abiding citizens at a disadvantage in a society where criminals run rampant and are supported by government. The idea here is to make Conservatives conform to Democrat policy by leveraging fear and trying to create, in them, a sense of helplessness. If the progressive ideology can appear overwhelmingly powerful, freedom-loving Americans might give in and give up the fight to preserve their freedom. Democrats are used to doing this with *their* voters like we see with the abortion cause, but scaring Conservatives doesn't work quite the same way.

Immediately after President Trump declared a national emergency to build a southern border wall, Nancy Pelosi used the 2nd amendment as leverage to fear Republicans into abandoning President Trump. She said:

"If the President can declare an emergency on something that he has created as an emergency, an illusion that he wants to convey, just think of what a President with different values can present to the American people. You want to talk about a national emergency? Let's talk about today, the one-year anniversary of another manifestation of the epidemic of gun-violence in America. That's a national emergency. Why don't you declare that an emergency Mr. President? I wish you would. But a Democratic President can do that. A Democratic President can declare emergencies as well."

Without saying it, Nancy Pelosi, made a veiled reference to the 2nd Amendment and gun-rights. The intent here appears to be to put fear in the hearts of gun-owners and those who support the 2nd Amendment. She knew better than to come out and say, *"If you build the wall, we will attack the 2nd Amendment"* because it would make it obvious that she and the Democrats were desperate at the time President Trump declared a national emergency to move forward on the border wall. In her speech, she went on to say,

"So the precedent that the President is setting here is something that should be met with great unease and dismay by the Republicans and of course we will respond accordingly when we review our options."

The *"should be met with great unease and dismay"* portion of her comment would seem to be wishful thinking on Pelosi's part but if she can make people scared of losing the 2nd Amendment as badly as her party has scared liberals of losing their government privilege of abortion, her goal with this speech would have been accomplished. Nancy may think she could gain political leverage over Donald Trump with this tactic but conservative-minded people can't be manipulated into giving up their freedom that easily. The intended result of Pelosi's 2nd Amendment scare tactic is that Republicans will put the pressure on Donald Trump and make him abandon his border wall. Democrats are so desperate for a larger voter base that they will use the 2nd Amendment to do it. They know how important the right to keep and bear arms is to Republicans, Conservatives and Trump supporters.

Let's go off the gun topic again for just a minute to clarify the political struggle behind the southern border wall. President Trump claims that drugs, gangs and other undesirables are coming through the open border and although that may be true, I want to focus on the political aspect of the wall. I am taking a leap of faith here because I can't see what will happen in the years to come with respect to the wall but this writing will be locked into history and we will see if I was correct. At this point, I don't even know if the wall actually gets built.

During this time of political strategy around the southern border wall (February 2019) both parties are looking 2-3 elections down the road and issues like abortion and gun-rights are the perfect tools to gain leverage because voters on both sides of the political isle are particularly passionate about these two topics. Ultimately, Democrats want to be able to give citizenship to as many illegal aliens as possible, as soon as possible. The constant flow of illegal immigrants into America will perfectly set up the Democrats for when the time comes. According to Nancy Pelosi, *"A Democratic President can declare emergencies as well."* Are we supposed to think a granting of mass-citizenship, to enhance the Democrat's voting base wouldn't happen? My guess is that as soon as Democrats are able, they will naturalize as many illegal immigrant voters as possible. Once they do, their campaign slogan will be, *"We fought for your citizenship, now you vote for us."* President Trump knows this and he is trying to stop it before it happens. Although he wants to keep the country safe from violence and drugs, he is also preventing America from plummeting into a socialist hell-hole 2-3 voting cycles down the road. That is the real reason he is pushing for the border wall.

People think Democrat opposition to the wall is to deny President Trump a victory. That may only be part of it. When Democrats decided a wall was immoral, it was around the same time they realized they could stay in power by using illegal immigrants who could be potentially converted into voters. This is when they stopped marketing to the white middle class and jumped on board with every social justice cause and minority group they could dig up. In fact, they have demonized the average white American citizen and work hard every day to plague them with the nomenclature of "white privilege." By utilizing all groups *other than* the middle class white voter, they could essentially out-vote traditional America. They know that

30-40 million people can sway an election either way and illegals are a perfect fit, if they could continue the flow for a few more years. What do you think will happen to the voting status of illegals in America if Democrats get power again?

In order to defeat traditional America, Socialist-Democrats need their supporters to kneel at the altar of politics. With the rise of socialism within the Democratic party and the demonization of traditional white Americans, Democrats may be able to transform America into the socialist Utopia they dream of. If we let them. The attack on our freedom is not coming down on us solely at the national level. State bureaucrats are working hard to violate the rights of those they work for as well. They often do it by shaming their constituents into going along with dangerous anti-American policies. They'll often use derogatory and insulting rhetoric toward the people they have been hired to represent.

While the citizens of Alabama seek to regain their God-given right to defend themselves, anti-gun politicians use delusional arguments to thwart their efforts. Senator Vivian Davis Figures accused the Alabama citizens she represents of having mental problems for wanting Constitutional Carry in their state. After a clear understanding of the bill in question, it would seem the Senator is a bit misguided and may have some mental problems of her own.

SB4 (otherwise known as a Constitutional Carry Bill) is welcomed by gun-owners across the state of Alabama, primarily because of the way it would prevent good people from being cornered by over-zealous gun-grabbers. The handgun permit system currently in place requires a permit in vehicles but not outside vehicles often turning law-abiding citizens into law breakers for simply traveling to the grocery store.

Paul Arnold from BamaCarry (an organization defending gun rights in Alabama) said, "SB4 makes the permit process optional but does not do away with the permit system or background checks at the time of purchase."

Arnold also said, "98% of BamaCarry members would still acquire a handgun permit for reciprocating purposes while traveling or purchasing a new firearm."

This doesn't stop the rhetoric from the agenda-driven Senator as she laid on a heaping helping of fearful, misleading anti-gun propaganda. Let's look at what Senator Vivian Davis Figures said in a committee hearing on SB4.

Senator Figures said, *"Why would you want to do certain things that really put people at greater risk?"*

Clearly, Senator Figures doesn't understand that SB4 does not eliminate background checks and in no way puts people at risk, but in typical anti-gun fashion, she uses the fear-campaign as a desperate attempt to get people on board to oppose the bill. Her statement also implies that anyone who votes for SB4 would be "putting people at greater risk." A typical shaming tactic often used by the gun-grabbers. This is similar to the "blood is on your hands" accusation often thrown at gun-owners.

Senator Figures said, *"You even want to repeal a part of the law that's in place now about carrying weapons into a demonstration, where everyone knows that the emotions are high,"*

This statement was particularly disturbing because it reveals very little about Alabama gun-owners and more about Senator Figures herself. This was her Freudian slip moment. The implication here is that *"when emotions are high, people will shoot each other."* When Freud talked about "Projection" he explains it as a way of people placing their own inner-most personal thoughts onto others. He said it was a way for people to blame others for thoughts that were occurring in their own mind. In this case it appears that Figures believes people will be unable to control themselves when emotions are high. Maybe Figures is revealing more about herself than she would like her voters to know. How would she be able to assume others would act out in an emotionally-reactive way if she wasn't already intimate with that very problem? Maybe Senator Figures doesn't trust others with guns because she wouldn't trust herself with a gun.

The idea that someone would think a gun could make people do violent things is a disturbing look into their thought-process and may expose more about them than the people they are accusing.

Senator Figures said, *"I've always gotten an 'F' from the National Rifle Association and that's a proud 'F' that I receive... I just don't understand the mentality of what you guys or – or what you guys continue to push to do,"* she said. *"Particularly, with all the gun violence that is happening, to allow a person to be able to get a gun who has mental problems – to me that says the person who's pushing that has some mental problems. They don't understand why people with mental issues shouldn't have a weapon."*

This statement rambled a bit but a few key points practically jump off the page. When she states she just doesn't *"understand the mentality of you guys,"* she seems to be saying that she has her view and all else is irrelevant. Then she threw in the ever-popular "gun-violence" term just to remind everyone that guns are the *cause* of violence. This is often used to re-direct anyone who might want to actually place the blame on the person pulling the trigger. Can't have that. If people realized violence is a human thing, we might force politicians to look at some of their own failed policies.

Then Figures attacks the citizens of Alabama again by restating they have mental problems but she also implies that SB4 would allow mentally-disabled people the ability to purchase guns. The bill, does not do that but like all true anti-gun politicians, Figures doesn't let those pesky facts get in the way of her mission to disarm the people she works for.

As of June 2019, 17 States already have Constitutional Carry in place without incident. That's the part the Anti-2nd Amendment Radicals hate, because it shows their argument for gun-restrictions to be irrational.

4. ANTI-GUN CULTISM

The biggest part of being brainwashed is not knowing
you are brainwashed.

Once your beliefs have been changed at the core level it
doesn't matter what data is presented to you. Your brain will
refute and deny anything that doesn't support the current belief
system. This is why cult members never believe that they are in
a cult. They are often taught that the reason the world
denounces them is because "they just don't understand." The
first and most important belief that must be anchored into a
person you want full control of, is the belief that they are doing
the right thing and *everyone else* is wrong. This gives them license
to condemn others in the name of justice while feeling a sense
of pride and righteousness. They believe they are the "Good
Guys." They must also believe that everyone else will try to tear
them down because the outside world is the enemy. They are
taught to believe evil will always be pursuing them but they
must remain strong in their fight to uphold the truth because
they are the honorable ones and the work they do will save
lives or improve humanity. They believe they must resist all
opposition.

But the truth is that they, the justice warriors, are the ones
being manipulated. This cult-strategy is used consistently on
liberal-progressives and heavily on recruits for the gun-control
mission. This is why Anti-Gunners believe they're doing the
right thing when they spew angry hateful misguided anti-gun
rhetoric, even when the facts and data show them the exact
opposite.

When you hear Anti-Gunners talking about guns, half of them know they are lying and the other half think they are telling the truth. But none of them are accurate because they've been conditioned to follow a very well-formulated anti-gun narrative and most are fresh out of the media's anti-gun graduate program. They can't help believing that guns are the cause of violence and gun-owners are evil because their thought-process is consistently (albeit subtly) cultivated to believe this at the core level.

If you continually teach your puppy to sit by using the tools of reward, he will eventually learn to sit. He will believe he is doing the "right" thing because he is rewarded when he sits. If you scold your puppy for chewing your slippers, he will most likely associate pain with the slippers and avoid them at all costs. Anti-Gunners are rewarded when they spread the anti-gun message by the feeling they get that they are saving lives. They feel good about themselves. The gun-control warriors are also rewarded within their peer-group through adulation and praise when they put themselves "out there" and oppose those evil NRA members. They avoid association with gun-owners because their peers make it perfectly clear that gun-owners are reckless and barbaric. The added tools that are used on people to keep them on the anti-gun bandwagon are fear and hate. Anti-2nd Amendment Radicals encourage fear of guns and hatred toward gun-owners. Fear and hate are the strongest human emotions and work very well when controlling the thoughts and actions of emotionally reactive people. For more on this, read the "Fear and Hate" chapter in Good Gun Bad Guy 2.

What does it take to get otherwise smart people to do things that most would consider "out of the realm of normal behavior?"

David Koresh was able to convince adults to burn alive in a fire along with their children in support of their mission. Regardless of your opinion or political position on the deadly fire in Waco, Texas, the truth remains that Koresh's followers could have escaped or given themselves up to the cops to save their own lives. They didn't because their devotion to the cause was stronger than the value of their lives or the lives of their children. It was their choice to stay. They chose a higher value to them at the time. Similar to the position some people have on abortion, when given the choice, some will sacrifice the life of a child in support of a "woman's right to choose." They choose the higher value to them. There has to be a good amount of mental leverage involved when someone can see a way to save their life or the life of their unborn child and not take it. Many people would look at either one of these situations and say, "the value of life is the highest value," but some don't see it that way.

The political hold the feminist movement has on people is strong. Should someone stray or go against the group's mission, they will be met with strong disapproval and punishment; often public shaming and sometimes even physical attacks. A big part of the movement is the demonizing of men. In order for this group to have a distinctive level of validation, they need an enemy. Men have been positioned as that enemy. The same is true for those among the radical anti-gun crowd. You'd better not get caught at the gun shop or even getting information on firearms if your anti-gun peers consider you a devout gun-grabber. If you are seen at the range or gathering gun information for any purpose other than improving the anti-gun argument, you will be swiftly corrected. Gun-owners are positioned as the enemy.

Charles Manson was able to convince people to kill on his behalf. Did these people already have the desire to kill in cold blood before they met Manson? Not even close. Leslie Van Houten was Homecoming Queen and studied to be a legal secretary before joining the Manson cult. Van Houten is a perfect example of someone vying for acceptance and willing to assist in a murder to get it. Van Houten desperately needed to be accepted by Manson and others in the group and when she was refused it and shunned, she became more willing to take part in the horrific act of murder. To some, acceptance is so important that they lose sight of the value of life. Manson preyed upon the weak-minded Van Houten and was able to manipulate her in ways no one else could. The mindset of those seeking validation, love and acceptance can often be easily exploited. These strategies are used in politics to sway public opinion and gather people who need to be part of a larger group.

Isn't it ironic how those on the left seem to agree on all the issues? How often do you find someone who is pro-choice and pro-gun? Conformity on the left is cultivated through schooling, media, movies and other societal influences. This type of group-think is simply not found on the right. If left to organic thought, people would gravitate toward beliefs that appeal to them individually and not what is served up at the popular table. More people could have values that actually cross political lines, but this does not equate to guaranteed votes so beliefs are cultivated from generation to generation as to ensure that people stay where they belong politically. Leverage is used when needed and righteousness is encouraged to simulate pride in the cause or agenda at hand.

The most important element of being brainwashed is believing that you could never be brainwashed.

You can tell the difference between an Anti-Gunner who has a political agenda and one who is just scared of guns. The

Anti-Gunner who is just scared of guns will typically let you know how they feel in a very passive way. In other words, they don't act confrontational. They usually want you to know how they feel about guns because they hope that a conversation with a gun-owner will ease their mind in some way. Maybe they will learn something they didn't know and will be able to develop a new understanding or gain some new information they can leave with that would help them feel better about guns.

I have always been afraid to fly. Maybe because I don't know enough about physics and can't understand how that monstrous thing stays in the air. A Boeing 747 weighs around 400,000 pounds and doesn't seem to be going all that fast at take-off. The problem is my lack of knowledge on the topic. That lack of information about engine thrust, velocity, aerodynamics and whatever other science is involved in keeping an airplane up, causes a certain level of fear for me when leaving the runway. Fear is always a result of a lack of information. Even though I fly a lot and have plenty of data that tells me thousands of planes fly every day without incident, I still don't enjoy it. So I talked to my friend Roger who is a commercial airline pilot, hoping to get some information that would help me.

It worked. He explained a lot of the physics behind flying and he explained his job, to a certain degree, in the cockpit. I did learn that there is a small window of time during take-off that he called "the point of no return." That wasn't very reassuring but he did say one thing that helped me out and it helps me every time I fly. He said, *"a commercial plane can take-off with only one engine."* That was important to me because it eased one huge fear I had. "Take-off" has always been the most uncomfortable part of the flight for me because it feels like the plane is pushing against every possible opposition and has more reasons to stay on the ground than float in the air.

I always thought from my limited perspective that both engines were necessary, especially at take-off because of symmetry and balance. If both engines *were* necessary, I could imagine all sorts of things going wrong that could potentially put an engine out. Given the fact that a commercial jet has two engines, the odds were twice as likely something could go wrong. Because of that simple bit of information from an expert, my fear level was significantly reduced. Now, having two engines is no longer a liability, but an asset in my mind.

So how does this relate to guns? Think about the lack of information most non-gun-owners walk around with every day. Not only is their sphere of knowledge limited, they are bombarded with inaccurate propaganda from left-wing media and politicians on a consistent basis. The anti-gun lobby is designed to brainwash people into a state of gun-fear and they are very good at it. If you are lucky enough to talk with an Anti-Gunner who *can* look at the topic of guns without a political bias, you have the opportunity to help them just like Roger helped me understand that flying wasn't nearly as dangerous as I made it out to be in my mind. It may be something as simple as the fact that on average, one out of twenty citizens are concealed carry license holders. Once they know this and they realize that they are in public with these people every day without incident, they may relax a bit and start to look at gun ownership differently. If they are given information about how many lives are saved by guns every year, they may even start to appreciate gun-ownership. Remember though, politicians and anti-gun media are working hard in the opposite direction every single day. Their goal is to erase any good work we do. Why? Because their mission is the exact opposite of ours. Freedom is the enemy of those who want a controlled society.

What about the Anti-Gunners *with* a political agenda? This is a different animal. I call them the Anti-2nd Amendment Radicals. Unlike the Anti-Gunner *without* a political agenda, the Anti-Gunner *with* a political agenda (Anti-2nd Amendment Radical) does not want to hear your logic. As a matter of fact, they work to cover up your information with lies because their intent is to stay "anti-gun." They don't want their opinion to change because it would reflect poorly on their previous judgment. They are smart enough to understand that the truth contradicts their narrative and they aren't really looking to fix any misconceptions. They are intent on *building* misconceptions to push for more gun-restrictions. You can tell them all day long that guns are used far more often to save lives than to take them, but rather than consider that fact, they will try to defeat your position in an effort to support their own. They need to win the argument because the outcome reflects on them personally. They do take it personally and will do anything they can to look good to whomever is watching. They don't care about saving lives. They don't feel sad when people are killed. They actually use gun-related tragedies to further their mission.

So, how does someone get like this? How do they become brainwashed on this topic to the point they will put people in danger or use killings to support their position? Very much in the same way Charles Manson and David Koresh's followers were manipulated. Anti-2nd Amendment Radicals and politically driven. Anti-Gunners are motivated by fear, political leverage, hate and a sense of righteousness.

Leslie Von Houten assisted in the death of innocent people in support of the mission and to gain acceptance from Charles Manson. Anti-2nd Amendment Radicals put good people in

85

danger with gun-restrictions in support of the mission and to stay in good graces with their peers on the left. Some, believe they are the good guys, defending innocent lives, while some believe they are the good guys, defending the mission of the Left. Both are dangerous because they believe they are the "good guys" in this fight. The anti-gun lobby invests millions each year into changing the way people think about guns in America. It's our job, whether we like it or not, to help them understand or defeat them at their game.

So, what causes this type of "locked in" mentality? How does the anti-gun position become so strong? First, we need to accept the fact that the gun debate is a battle within a war. Those on the left, want government control over society for a number of different reasons we don't have to get into at the moment and guns are one obstacle to that goal. People on the right, want freedom to live their lives on their own terms. The problem occurs when influential figures polarize the two groups in the pursuit of political power. Most often, people don't even recognize what is being done to them and just fight the battle with everything they have. Similar to brainwashing, in order to get people to fight for a cause or mission, their beliefs must be fundamentally changed or locked in. But what's to stop them from forming new beliefs and changing course? To keep someone married to a mission, there must be some form of consistent leverage.

Let's say we have an anti-gun activist. You know the type. They sneer every time someone walks into the room wearing anything that represents America. If they see an image of a gun on a shirt or hat, they quickly leave, out of fear there will be a shoot-out or they sarcastically question the "need" for wearing something so offensive. If you somehow get engaged in a conversation, they will make sure to tell you how "nobody needs an AR-15." They are not only full of gun fear, they are enraged at you, the Conservative, for many reasons. They believe they are above you intellectually, they consider you a danger to society and they believe you are ignorant to the way the world really works. They think they are on the cutting edge of a more culturally-sophisticated, evolved, progressive society and you are a bumbling hillbilly clinging to old values while putting everyone in danger. They believe you are getting in the way of progress. If they get the chance, they will tell you that your views are "antiquated," your logic is "flawed" and you need to be more "diverse."

We know it is unlikely that they will change their position but what keeps them there is the most interesting part of the brainwashing. For people to truly believe that they are better, smarter and more sophisticated than others, there has to be some underlying mechanisms put into place. This type of behavior doesn't just happen.

The entire liberal-progressive belief structure is anchored by two psychological components; intellectual superiority and moral superiority with a resistance to ideas that fall outside their political doctrine.

Later on I will discuss how to dissect these fabricated beliefs but first, let's explore how they are developed.

Ever since Kayla was born, she was taught that she was highly intelligent. She was taught to believe that she was advanced far beyond other students but she was never to flaunt this gift of intellectual superiority. She was taught to help others who were not quite as advanced as her. After all, not everyone could be as special as Kayla. In order for Kayla to maintain this gift and the reputation it afforded her and her family, she could never waiver in her school work. Kayla would go on to the most prestigious college and her family would consistently reinforce the notion that she was far superior to others. Kayla's parents would grease the college wheels when necessary with a healthy donation or an incentive to those who helped the family maintain Kayla's prestigious persona and high grades. Kayla's parents even paid administrators to qualify Kayla when her grades didn't meet the level needed to attend the prestigious university of choice.

Throughout Kayla's life, she was also taught that there were many people in America that were less fortunate than she. She was taught to believe that she had an inherent privilege that others just didn't have. In Kayla's mind, these people were much less evolved on an intellectual level but also lack in moral character and are often unable to make their way financially. They often can't make the right choices in life because they don't have the moral compass that Kayla has or they don't have the resources due to society strategically holding them back. Because Kayla was taught to believe that she was better than most people, she developed a sense of moral superiority. She was told she should teach these people that just because they didn't share the same financial ability as her, it didn't mean they shouldn't be able to enjoy some of the benefits they were entitled to. Kayla learned to feel good about herself when she supported causes that helped the morally, intellectually and financially deprived people of society. She pretended she wasn't any better than them, but she always felt as though she was.

Kayla was also taught that there were people in America that didn't care about helping the "victims of society." They would expect them to earn their own way and when criminals broke the law, this mean group of people would want to throw them in prison. This mean group ran around with guns, drove vehicles that destroyed the environment and prayed to some silly God. They also tried to tell Kayla that she didn't have the right to "choose" her career over an insignificant "clump of cells" that developed in her body. Kayla was consistently reinforced to believe that her views of the world were correct and those who disagreed with her, just didn't understand, or worse, wanted to hold back progress. Kayla's parents and professors would teach her how the world really worked and when the time was right they would take the beliefs they instilled in her and attach to them a sense of anger and righteousness. Kayla would soon feel the need to speak out and demand that social justice be had for all the people in the world, regardless of the dangerous effects it would bring. Kayla would believe that those evil conservatives trying to halt progress, must be stopped. She was taught that above all, she must RESIST.

Throughout Kayla's life she was taught that government was in charge. There were laws, rules and restrictions for a reason. The people who ran government were looking out for the best interest of others and those crazy conservative people who thought they knew better, were living in the past and creating dangerous situations for everyone. As Kayla got older, she was consistently reinforced by her professors, family, friends and media that guns had no place in this progressive society and were only a bi-product of an outdated belief that the country should adhere to a ridiculous document call the Constitution. This made perfect sense to Kayla because the argument she always heard was that if there were no guns, no one could get shot. She learned to believe that gun-owners are mostly irresponsible and if more restrictions were placed on them, more lives could be saved.

Kayla wanted to be the one responsible for saving lives. Kayla was never given the whole story so when she would hear contradicting views on the topic of guns, she couldn't accept it. Her brain wouldn't comprehend a view that claimed the exact opposite of the one she had heard her entire life. Remember, the people opposing her gun-position were the same ones who were running around with guns, recklessly and intentionally putting everyone in danger. They could never be trusted; so how could she ever take them seriously. Besides, if Kayla were to consider the pro-gun position it would mean that the people she loved and respected would have given her inaccurate information. It would also mean that Kayla had been wrong for all these years and that just couldn't be. She went to the best college and was far more intellectually superior than everyone else. Rather than try to understand different views, Kayla chose to RESIST them.

How could all the people who influenced Kayla her entire life be wrong? How could Kayla be wrong? Even worse, how could these terrible and intellectually-deficient conservatives be correct? Kayla would need to solidify her anti-gun position and eliminate the possibility of any opposing view being accurate. Kayla would take her anti-gun position and double down because in her mind, she knew she was smarter and of a much higher moral-integrity than others.

Kayla would soon learn to fight ferociously against those who purposely wanted to endanger society with guns and she found groups of people just like her who felt the same way. The more she spoke out, the more opposition she received, and the angrier she would get. She would also receive abundant support from her fellow Anti-Gun Radicals. They would tell her to keep fighting and that she was doing the moral thing. They would tell her that every time she angered a gun-owner, she was saving innocent lives. Opposition became her motivator. Resistance made her feel strong. Kayla's activism would grow in intensity and she would become even more righteous in her position. Kayla knew with every bit of her soul that she was doing the right thing because she was told that when "they" would get mad, she was winning. Kayla believes she is one of the "good guys." Kayla knows that she is smarter and morally-superior than others so she must be right when it comes to the gun-conversation...even though Kayla has never seen a real gun up close.

Unfortunately, this is what happens to some. This is the brainwashing that occurs. These are the people lobbying politicians to legislate away your rights. They have positioned you as the enemy and themselves as "intellectually" and "morally" superiority. They have had rock solid psychological leverage performed on them for a very long time. "Facts" and "statistics" most often mean nothing to these people. When the facts *are* important, only *their* "facts" are relevant.

The irrational fear of guns, perpetuated by the anti-gun left, has worked its way into our society in such a way that causes people to take extreme action on situations that exist only in their minds. Oftentimes, when guns are the topic of discussion, those of the anti-gun mindset, believe their fantasies over the stark contrast of what is actually occurring in the real world. It's so bad that the mere photo of a gun, a Pop-Tart chewed into the shape of a gun or someone making a hand gesture that looks like a gun has become cause for alarm among those who have this condition. These irrational views are perpetuated by gun-fear-groups like Moms Demand Action and other anti-gun lobbying organizations.

The knee-jerk reaction to anything gun-related comes from people who have been cultivated to fear guns through concerted propaganda and rhetoric. The people who fall for this type of fear-campaign seem to be very illogical, irrational and emotionally driven when it comes to the topic of guns. These are often people who have never even held a gun in their hands. Critical thinking gets thrown out the window in exchange for dangerous, reactive emotion. Let's not forget the hypocrisy.

Does the hypocrisy of the Anti-Gun crowd make you wonder if they're actually capable of rational thought? For example, have you ever heard them say, "Nobody needs an AR-15," or "Nobody needs a gun in their home," or "Nobody needs to carry a gun in public." The implication is that if you don't "need" a gun, you shouldn't have one. As if they were the ones to grant you your God given right, based on "their" interpretation of need. The Anti-Gunners say these things to sway public opinion and make gun-ownership look unreasonable. But let's look at some numbers and talk about the "need" to own a gun. Now we all know that the Founders didn't call the Constitutional Amendments, the "Bill of Needs" and although we know that gun-ownership is our right, there may be a significant argument to be made for the need to carry a gun. In our home, at the grocery store or anywhere else for that matter.

According to a study by Gary Kleck with confirming data from the CDC, there are approximately 2.5 million defensive gun uses in America every year. That means 2.5 million potential lives saved because people had guns in their possession when they were attacked. 46% of those were women. That doesn't necessarily mean Good Guys killing Bad Guys. It most often meant the mere presence of a gun deterred an attacker. In other words,

"The attacker knew his potential victim had a gun, and chose not to attack."

There are just over 300 million people in America (326,000,000 in 2017). There are just over 1 million successful
92

violent crimes in America per year (1,248,580 in 2017 / FBI data). 300 million people/1 million attacks. That's a 1 in 300 chance that you'll be the victim of one of those attacks. I don't know about you, but I don't like those odds. The Anti-Gunners will tell you, it'll never happen to them, yet many of these same people will buy lottery tickets with a 1 in 20 million chance of winning because, "You gotta be in it to win it." There's the hypocrisy.

Twice as many violent attacks are prevented than carried out, because the victim had a gun.

Question 1: What would the result be if more people were denied their right to carry a gun?

Question 2: What would the result be if more people exercised their right to carry?

Many of these Anti-Gunners will tell you that their odds of being attacked are far less likely because they don't live in the bad part of town, yet they govern those parts of town through the politicians they vote for. The thing the Anti-Gunners ignore is, if their odds of being the victim in a violent attack go down, someone else's odds have to go up because the number of people didn't change and the number of yearly attacks didn't change. They'll tell you that we need more gun-restrictions while watching innocent people die in high crime areas and gun free zones. There's more of their hypocrisy.

Rather than admit to the world that gun-ownership is a right and also a need, the gun-grabbers pretend they have no blood on their hands while using the death-toll numbers from high crime areas to push for more gun-control. They stand on the graves of those they have put in harm's way and they use anti-gun propaganda to fool people who aren't paying attention, into believing that they care. Human-violence in America is not an argument for more gun-restrictions, it's an argument for more armed-preparedness and firearms training.

What is the left trying to accomplish with their anti-gun brainwashing?

In Colorado, 16-year-old Loveland High School Junior, Nathan Myers, was kicked out of school and told not to come back until the school was able to "conduct an investigation," into what they called, a threatening Snapchat by the student. The short video consisted of footage of firearms in their cases that Nathan took during an innocent day of shooting with his family. The guns were very well-kept and frankly not a bad collection. However, those in charge at the school decided that this was a threatening video and Nathan should be investigated, causing Nathan's Father to prove his innocence to the police. The student who reported the Snapchat video claimed to be scared that Nathan would "shoot up the school." This is the result of the anti-gun left and their misguided fear. It's working exactly as the Anti-2nd Amendment Radicals planned, but the people at the Thompson Valley School can't see that they, and others like them, are the ones who have been manipulated. Thompson Valley School District spokesman, Michael Hausmann, refused to comment on the school's horrible accusations.

In another delusional cry for gun-control, a Pennsylvania man was convicted of disorderly conduct for making a shooting gesture with his hand. Stephen Kirchner, in response to his neighbor "giving him the finger," replied with a hand gesture that simulated a gun. The delusional neighbor told authorities he felt "extremely threatened" by the gesture and

Kirchner was found "at fault." You read that right. The neighbor "felt" threatened by someone pointing their finger like a gun. It's clear that something is happening to a group of people in our society, but what is it?

According to the Cleveland Clinic website:

"Delusional disorder, previously called paranoid disorder, is a type of serious mental illness — called a "psychosis"— in which a person cannot tell what is real from what is imagined. The main feature of this disorder is the presence of delusions, which are unshakable beliefs in something untrue."

"These delusions usually involve the misinterpretation of perceptions or experiences. In reality, however, the situations are either not true at all or highly exaggerated."

"People with delusional disorder often can continue to socialize and function quite normally, apart from the subject of their delusion, and generally do not behave in an obviously odd or bizarre manner."

"In some cases, however, people with delusional disorder might become so preoccupied with their delusions that their lives are disrupted."

Anti-Gun "Delusional Disorder" has been cultivated over many years. Just in time for "Red Flag Laws." More on Red Flag Laws in the next chapter.

Whenever we hear from the anti-gun crowd, it's usually because they want to lecture us on something they know nothing about. We sometimes just find ourselves rolling our eyes because we can see their ignorance but we know we may never be able to help *them* see it. Typically, when people feel the need to lecture you on a topic, their motivation is emotionally driven. They are looking to either change your mind so they feel justified in their position or they want to stump you so they feel like they have won. We don't really know what it is exactly that they win, but they sure do need it. This may go back to the idea that if they can win the argument by resisting your views, somehow they are smarter than you. This is important to some people.

Resistance to ideas other than theirs is an interesting (and somewhat sad) strategy used by the anti-American crowd. The resistance, in and of itself massages their belief that they are saving the world. ..."doing something," as it were. Demonstrable results, logic or a supposed goal of saving lives be damned - being oppositional and contrarian are their raisons d'être. Their self-worth is so tied up in their "the sky is green jello and birds don't eat worms," beliefs that they must argue for those beliefs. Little do they realize that "resistance" eats them alive. When people "resist," they are inserting their will against the natural flow of life. They believe their resistance is actually stopping something in the outside world, but in reality they are resisting something that has either already happened in the past or something they think will happen in the future. The effects of resistance, live only in the minds of those doing the resisting. Because resistance is a mental stance, it has no effect on the outside world. Resistance does however affect the Resistor in ways that deteriorate the ability to think rationally. The inner-resistance to an event does not actually change the event from occurring but it does build anger and anxiety within the mind of the person trying to change the outside world with internal will.

If someone expresses an idea or belief, resistance does absolutely nothing to stop them from having said it because it already happened in the past. If someone will express an idea or belief five minutes from now, resistance to that idea or belief will do nothing to stop them from expressing it in the future. RESISTANCE, although pushed heavily as a political tool does nothing but create turmoil within those who are foolish enough to try and use it as a way of implementing change. Resistance is really an attempt at preventing an event from happening in our own minds. In other words, "if I resist an idea or oppose something that already happened or could happen in the future, I may be able to eliminate the experience of that thing in my own mind." Resistance is a form of internal denial that has no effect on the outside world. "Resistance" does seem to create a sense of anger, hostility and even physical tension in those who use it. There was a whole movement created around the RESIST idea in 2016 but many have abandoned it. Abandoning the resistance strategy may have been an attempt to reduce their own level of stress and anxiety after seeing that the only thing their RESISTANCE managed to accomplish was physically visible distress and health issues.

Many people on the anti-gun bandwagon have realized that simply resisting Pro-Gunners is mentally unhealthy so they have developed strategies to combat the idea of the 2nd Amendment but because their argument has no validity, their position must be based purely on rhetoric and inaccurate information.

Anti-Gunners will never enter a conversation on guns without having some facts (or what they think are facts) ready to go. They may have a few statistics they saw in a Moms Demand Tweet or a catch-phrase like *"The NRA has blood on their hands for selling assault weapons to children."* Sometimes they'll try to present the argument originally presented by their beloved President Obama that *"We flood communities with so many guns that it is easier for a teenager to buy a Glock than get his hands on a computer or even a book."*

Regardless of their strategy when they enter into a conversation about guns, the typical Anti-Gunner is usually working with information that has been created to indoctrinate *them* into the anti-gun camp. The information is not usually worthy of debate because it has no substance or relevance due to its inaccuracy. Remember, they didn't hear it on liberal media so they would have better tools to argue their case. They heard it because it was a tool being used *on them* for the purpose of getting them on-board. This is why their arguments are most often based in emotion. It's what motivated them in the first place and they are now trying to use it on you. Remember, the arguments they use on you are emotional arguments that worked on THEM.

"Why do you need to take a gun to a soccer game?"

This and other similar questions are asked to make the gun-owner feel ashamed or embarrassed. The Anti-Gunner thinks the Pro-Gunner will be ashamed or embarrassed because *they* would be if they were asked the question. The implication is:

1. *The gun-owner is always scared for their life.* The Anti-Gunner uses the word "need" a lot because the only reason they can imagine carrying a gun is out of fear, therefore, they believe everyone else carries out of fear. They can't see this from the gun-owners perspective because they have never known it first-hand. In other words, carrying out of a sense of responsibility is a perspective they are blind to. They imagine gun-owners to be constantly looking over their shoulder out of fear. They project their own thoughts on others

2. *The gun-owner is ruining the mood of an otherwise peaceful, fun event.* Somehow the gun-owner is supposed to feel like they are ruining the party by having a gun. To the Anti-Gunner, a gun is a buzz-kill because it represents death and danger, plus if they know a gun is in their presence, it's all they can think about. So, in a sense, guns do ruin the mood for Anti-Gunners, but it's only because of their irrational fear of them; whereas a gun-owner will have a much more comfortable time at an event knowing that they have a gun on them because they know they are capable of protecting themselves and those around them.

3. *The gun-owner is putting people in danger because they are bringing a gun to a public venue.* The Anti-Gunner has a very difficult time seeing a gun as something that could keep people safe. Whenever a gun is around, Anti-Gunners fear the gun accidentally "going off" or the gun-owner becoming irate and killing people because they can't control their emotions. This is purely projection on the part of the Anti-Gunner because they believe all people have a tendency to act irrationally. Again, they fail to see the concept that most people can actually control themselves.

Mindy Morelaw: Why do you need to take a gun to a soccer game?

B. A. Freeman: Because my life is no less valuable at a soccer game.

Mindy Morelaw: I'm not saying it is, I just don't think it's necessary to put everyone in danger.

B. A. Freeman: The only way people would be in danger because of my gun is if I chose to be irresponsible. Do you expect me to be irresponsible?

Mindy Morelaw: For all I know, you could be crazy. And I don't want to be around crazy people.

B. A. Freeman: So if I didn't have my gun, would you feel safer?

Mindy Morelaw: Yes.

B. A. Freeman: How many people would you say are at this soccer game right now?

Mindy Morelaw: I don't know. Six hundred maybe?

B. A. Freeman: If there was a law that prevented me from having my gun with me today, there is a good chance that someone who wanted to do harm to others would pay no attention to that law. The idea that everyone would obey the law is a fairytale. That law would put you in more danger because someone like me, who has good intentions would be rendered unarmed and helpless.

Mindy Morelaw: Yeah, but I don't know for sure that your intentions are good. I do know that there are some very bad people out there and if they are allowed to have guns, it could get people killed. If there was a law, it could prevent dangerous people from owning guns.

B. A. Freeman: But that would assume that the bad guys would follow the law. Right?

Mindy Morelaw: I think most would follow the law.

B. A. Freeman: Let's assume, most would. Look at this crowd. Which ones are the bad guys?

Mindy Morelaw: How am I supposed to know?

B. A. Freeman: Exactly. You wouldn't. You could never know. But gun laws would assure you of one thing.

Mindy Morelaw: What's that?

B. A. Freeman: That I wouldn't be armed.

Mindy Morelaw: Yeah but I don't know if you are one of the good guys.

B. A. Freeman: It wouldn't matter because the good guys would be the only ones disarmed. You would be essentially weeding out all the people who could protect you. You would also be sending a message to those who want to do harm that I am no longer a threat to them. Congratulations, your magical gun law just made you less safe.

Mindy Morelaw: Sometimes I think you gun-nuts blow the violence in America way out of proportion. I think you do it to make it seem like we all need to be running around with guns to save our own lives or something. I mean, what are the odds anyway that I'll be attacked by these violent people that you say are running around all over the place?

B. A. Freeman: Well, I never said that but, ok. Let me try to put things in perspective. How many people live in this country?

Mindy Morelaw: I don't know. 500 million or something? Who knows? A lot! Who cares?

B. A. Freeman: Well, you're a bit off. It's just over 300 million.

Mindy Morelaw: Ok...So?

B. A. Freeman: How many violent crimes are committed in America per year?

Mindy Morelaw: Oh, I know this one because I just saw a report on MSNBC. They said about a million.

B. A. Freeman: Close. It's just over 1 million, but let's call it a million for the sake of easy math. If there are around 300 million people in this country and approximately 1 million violent attacks per year, what are the odds that you could be one of those attack victims?

Mindy Morelaw: Um... I guess 1 in 300

B. A. Freeman: I don't like those odds. Do you?

Mindy Morelaw: It'll never happen! Those odds make it so unlikely that I will be attacked that I can guarantee it will never happen!

B. A. Freeman: Do you ever buy lottery tickets? You know, for fun?

Mindy Morelaw: Sure. You can't win it, unless you're in it!

B. A. Freeman: So you believe you have a chance? I mean, you're actually spending money on them, so you must believe there's a chance you'll win, right?

Mindy Morelaw: Yeah, sure. Why not me?

B. A. Freeman: Yes. That's right. Why not you? Did you know that the average odds of winning the lottery are 1 in 20 million?

Mindy Morelaw: Yeah, so?

B. A. Freeman: You believe you can win a lottery that offers you a 1 in 20 million chance, but you think you could never be attacked when the odds are only 1 in 300. You may want to ask yourself if there is something else influencing your thought-process.

Mindy Morelaw: Whatever...

Good Gun Bad Guy 3

5. RED FLAG LAWS

"Those who would give up essential liberty to purchase a little temporary safety, deserve neither liberty nor safety."

– Benjamin Franklin.

In the Preface, we talked about control. In August of 2019, as I write this chapter, Democrats and even some Republicans are entertaining the idea of Red Flag Laws. They are being pressured by a false narrative created by the media. Within two days, America endured two mass killings perpetrated by two separate lunatics with prominent left-wing ideological beliefs. The result, as usual, was not a call to fix the underlying societal problems and human-behavioral issues that caused the violent behavior, but a reactionary plea to "just do something" while simultaneously blaming the problem on President Trump and American gun-owners. The problem is, those who react without thinking, will always gravitate toward a "quick fix" to violent behavior and disregard the potential negative effects it may have on good people. Their solution to violence: RED FLAG LAWS.

Red Flag Laws have been implemented by several states and have proven to be a disaster in the way they violate the rights of good people, put them in physical danger, leave them unarmed and helpless and do nothing to stop Bad Guys; all under the guise of "keeping guns out of the hands of mentally deranged individuals." Now the Gun-Grabbers want to implement Red Flag Laws on a national level.

Gary Willis was a sixty year old man from Maryland who was shot and killed by cops in his own home because a family member told them that he could be a risk. Red Flag Laws, also known as Extreme Risk Protection Orders (ERPO) turn police against the people and give police departments the authority to confiscate guns without due process.

Gary's death happened solely because of an accusation. Red Flag Laws violate due-process and leave good people to defend themselves in court, prove their innocence and fight to get their rights back if they're not killed first. Gary's niece Michelle said this all stemmed from a family argument and Gary would never hurt anyone.

This is what our Founding Fathers warned us about. Red Flag Laws are an example of the tyranny they feared. This is why the 2nd Amendment was written. They may not have known exactly how government would strategically use its power over the people, but they had a sense that men without morals and drunk on control would take advantage of those who put them in office as soon as they could. Our founders saw these tyrannical gun-grabbers coming two hundred years away.

The most disgusting and disturbing thing about the loss of Gary Willis is that some Anti-Gunners and Anti-2nd Amendment Radicals are calling his death a success. Here are some responses to the unjustified death of Gary. You'll see the lack of compassion for an innocent man and a desire to win the gun debate at all costs.

TWITTER POST:
Ari Bargolani @AriBargolani – Nov 11
"@AACOPD just saw an example of your exemplary law enforcement. Good job! That's one person disarmed and that will not hurt anyone ever…"

TWITTER POST:
Ain't Tellin' How Much Longer @AAmelia98 – Nov 8
Replying to @GovLarry Hogan
"This is a good start to stop this from happening in our state"

In response to the idea of Red Flag Laws, Jonas Oransky, deputy legal director of Everytown for Gun Safety said, *"We think of this as a new frontier."* – Washington Post

---

The justification for gun-confiscation prior to the person committing a crime is that these terrible government over-reaches will prevent future crimes. Our system was not designed like that but the Anti-2nd Amendment Radicals don't care because it is a way for them to gain leverage of their political opponents under the guise of public safety. The groups who support these laws, laugh at the fact that the rights of real Americans are violated in the process of executing these gun-grabs. The mindless citizens behind the Anti-2nd Amendment groups don't care because they don't own guns and they welcome the control of government. You, the gun-owner, just get in the way of their Utopian dream and their vengeful hatred of your freedom.

The anti-gun-media-fear-campaign has not only plagued uninformed citizens but also many state officials across the country. Some Governors across the United States have packaged their own dangerous Red Flag Laws and the Anti-2nd

107

Amendment Radicals love this because it is a way for them to control those who oppose them politically. It's also a way for them to cover up corruption in politics. When they talk about "gun-violence," what they are really doing is re-directing your focus away from their failed policies. We know "gun-violence" is just a term created by the gun-grabbers that is designed to take the blame off of murderers and place it on guns and gun-owners. The term "gun-violence" is a mask for "human-violence."

If politicians were forced to talk about human-violence they would have to talk about their own failures; gang-violence, poverty, open borders, sanctuary cities, welfare dependency, politically motivated groups like Antifa and a nation of people dependent on pharmaceutical & street drugs. These are all problems that they create. So of course, they want you to think the problem is guns.

In just over a month since Maryland's Red Flag Law went into effect, 114 guns were confiscated without due-process and an innocent man (Gary Willis) was dead. Gun-grabbers call these laws "common sense." Why? Because they want everyone on board and using the term "common sense" as a way of shaming people into supporting these dangerous and irresponsible laws. Anti-gun leftists would rather be seen as having (self-proclaimed) common sense than have to admit that the policies they support are all wrong, because everything they do is a reflection on them and not really about the greater good as they would like you to believe. Notice that all the states with Red Flag Laws implemented at the time of this writing are Democrat run governments, drunk on power with voter support of people who want to be controlled. Those who support these laws are typically non-gun-owners and go unaffected in the short-term.

2019 States with Red Flag Laws include:

- Connecticut
- Indiana
- California
- Washington
- Oregon
- Colorado
- Florida
- Vermont
- Maryland
- Rhode Island
- New Jersey
- Delaware
- Massachusetts
- Illinois
- New York
- Nevada
- Hawaii

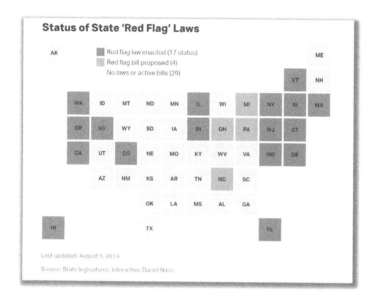

Status of State 'Red Flag' Laws

Red flag law enacted (17 states)
Red flag bill proposed (4)
No laws or active bills (29)

Last updated: August 5, 2019

Source: State legislatures. Interactive: Daniel Nass

Red Flag Laws get innocent people killed, violate due-process and use police departments to strong-arm law-abiding citizens. This is not how our American justice system was intended by our Founding Fathers. Red Flag Laws are dangerous to our society and our freedom regardless of party affiliation. Even the laughing and cheering gun-grabbers will pay the price for this when their government turns on them and violates their rights. Even though the senseless people who support these laws will eventually feel the effects of their sinister and irresponsible ways, we cannot allow these laws to stand. By the time real American say *"See we told you so,"* it will be too late. Unfortunately, for Gary Willis, it is already too late. We need to stop these reckless law makers and we need to help their supporters see that these laws are dangerous for everyone. Our future generations will look back at us and either thank us for defending their rights and freedom or they will wonder why we sat by and did nothing.

Along with the infamous Red Flag Laws, comes a long laundry list of other gun-restrictions Anti-2nd Amendment Radicals would like to put in place. We could talk about magazine capacity, concealed-carry restrictions, extended background checks, and so much more, but let's take a quick look at the left's desire to ban suppressors, or as they like to call them, "silencers."

Anti-2nd Amendment Radicals in congress want to ban suppressors. Why? Well, they'd like you to believe that suppressors encourage murderers to go on killing sprees because somehow their guns will magically become silent if a suppressor is used. They actually try calling them "silencers," hoping the term will catch on so they can fool the people who aren't paying attention. Those anti-gun folks who don't know any better, but know that they fear guns, will fall for anything if they are politically motivated or scared enough.

The truth is, criminals don't use suppressors because they're heavy, they make firearms much harder to hide and they don't quiet a gun nearly enough to justify their use in a crime, but that doesn't stop the anti-gun crowd from pushing the fake narrative about suppressors. Try telling an Anti-Gunner that suppressors are never used in mass killings and they will rebut with the one case in which a suppressor was found. They are trained to have the Virginia Beach killing ready-to-go, because it is the only one they know of where a suppressor was found at the scene. Hardly justification to ban the item, but remember, Anti-Gunners don't care about saving lives as much as they want to suppress YOU - and they will take advantage of any opportunity that presents itself.

The anti-gun crowd will act as though, had it not been for the suppressor, the killing would not have occurred. They will push the narrative that, if suppressors are banned, lives will be saved. I would argue that suppressors save lives, because if one's hearing is damaged, they may be a risk when driving or engaging in other activities that require acute auditory capability.

So what do suppressors do? They help protect the hearing of gun-owners, they reduce noise pollution (often important when hunting) and they can make firearms training more comfortable. Anti-Gunners don't care about your hearing, they hate the idea of hunting and they don't want you to be more proficient with your firearms, so none of these things matter to them.

Take an AR-15 for example, (one of the most commonly owned rifles in America.) Unsuppressed, the AR-15 produces about 165 decibels. A suppressed AR-15 will produce about 132 decibels. That's just below the CDC occupational hazard limit of 140 decibels but still louder than a Ted Nugent concert. A suppressed rifle is also louder than a siren and thunder, which both come in around 120 decibels.

So why do the dishonest Gun-Grabbers lie to you? Well, they're not trying to fool gun-owners because we won't buy their nonsense for a minute. They want to fool those who don't know any better. Gun Grabbers want to scare people into supporting their policies that further restrict the rights of their own fellow citizens. What better way to push laws through, than to scare people and make them believe that killers are out there roaming through neighborhoods, massacring people with suppressors and no one can even hear it happening?

Since Red Flag Laws give police departments the right to violate due process based on the notion that someone could be a "risk," wouldn't they be able to claim a person a "risk" if that person was harboring a suppressor that was deemed "illegal" by the same government that created the Red Flag Law?

Many Anti-Gunners are waking up to the lies of the anti-gun left. They are starting to realize that they've been fooled by the politicians they once trusted. Some are beginning to understand that if their political-puppet-masters will mislead them on this topic, it is quite possible that they have been and will be misled on many others. But this doesn't stop the Anti-2nd Amendment Radicals and their lobbying groups from constantly attacking the right to keep and bear arms. So although they hope to disarm law-abiding citizens, by implementing laws that violate your rights, they forget, that just like our guns, real Americans won't be silenced. But why are the politicians who represent us, so intent on making us subservient?

The right to keep and bear was written into The Bill of Rights as Amendment #2, but that doesn't mean people won't try to violate it. Unfortunately, our fight is against fellow Americans who think they know what is best for everyone. Their fear of what they don't understand and their lust for government control sends them down a destructive ideological path, which trades individual freedom for passive obedience.

Freedom is embraced by people with a rugged individualism fueled by the desire for growth, prosperity and the will to live life as they see fit. Along with this way of life, comes a strong sense of personal responsibility. When these people make a mistake, they take full responsibility for their failures. When these people succeed, they expect to reap the rewards of their success. These people understand that government was put into place to serve the needs of "the people." Let's call these people, "conservatives."

Socialism is embraced by people with a "group-think" mindset fueled by the desire for a structured, government-controlled society. This is the preferred model of people who want to "feel" safe in a world that they may not understand or have the courage to endure. This ideology seems to bring with it, a lack of personal responsibility. "It's always someone else's fault." This is the mindset of people who can trip over their own feet while walking down the sidewalk and find a way to justify suing the business that happens to be there. This is a mindset that embraces "victimhood" and would vote for the politician that promises handouts and college loan forgiveness, even while watching others work hard to pay their own way. These are people who believe it is ok to take from those who earn and give it to those who don't, under the guise of compassion. Let's call these people "progressives."

The political Left in America has flirted with the idea of socialism for decades but never admitted it in public, until recently. Some Democrats have jumped on the opportunity to sell the idea of socialism to anyone who might qualify themselves as a "victim" or "entitled." Not all Democrats are ready to admit their true desires just yet, but a small group of radicals can't seem to hold back. The old school Democrats know better than to publicly announce their agenda now because they are not ready to seize the moment effectively. The young, foolish radicals (and even a Bernie Sanders) are taking a defiant position against their old-school fellow party members as they scream their mission from the mountaintop.

This is a problem for the Democratic party because they know that they must have a few key elements in place before implementing socialism in America.

1. **They need more voters.**
   This is why Democrats abandoned the white, middle class, blue-collar voter and decided to pander to every minority group possible. They have done the math and have figured out that the white, middle-class, Republican/Conservative voter can eventually be out-voted. The formula is simple; befriend all minority groups, and create some if needed, while demonizing white people; but they need an open border to accomplish this. This is also why their position on the border changed so dramatically - practically overnight. Their motto would be, "we gave you all the benefits of citizenship, now you vote for us," with the implication that they can always be sent back if they don't stay loyal. Democrats don't necessarily want to convert illegals into citizens because they could start voting Republican once they see the truth. They do however, want illegals to have driver's licenses and voting rights as long as they identify as "Democrats." They desperately need the votes and President Trump knows it. The "Wall" is primarily for the purpose of denying Democrats the ability to turn illegal aliens into Democrat voters and preserving American freedom for future generations.

   They didn't expect Trump to come along and build a wall.

2. **They need dependent citizens.**

Democrats have been desperately denying the success of Trump's economy, while pushing the "doom and gloom" of college debt and the fake-narrative of "big corporations making the 'little guy' poor." Many have lived through college debt, but those who have been conditioned to see themselves as "victims of corporate oppression," don't believe they should be required to pay it back. This "entitlement" and "victimhood" breeds dependency. It is very important to Democrats that they keep as many people on the government dole as possible. The Democrat message is, "If you vote for those mean old Republicans, they will make you pay your own way. We will give you everything for free, just vote for us and support our tax increases."

The economy was supposed to continue its Obama-era decline, but Trump fixed it.

3. **They need the guns.**
   The big reason there is such a divide within the Democratic party right now is because the radical "Squad," consisting of Alexandria Ocasio-Cortez, Ilhan Omar, Ayanna Pressley and Rashida Tlaib have revealed the Democrat's true colors too soon. Some would argue that the "new push for gun-control" began in 1994 with the "assault weapons ban" and was intended to work hand-in-hand with the eventual push for socialism. The problem is, they were supposed to wait before actually attacking their fellow Americans with socialism, which is why there is now such a mad rush for "assault-rifle" bans, Red Flag Laws, universal background checks, ammo restrictions and countless

other 2nd Amendment violations. Nancy Pelosi and the old-school Democrats are not happy with the young new radicals (or the not-so-young ones with big mouths) because they are screwing up the "no one wants to take your guns" bait and switch.

They were supposed to get the guns first.

Red Flag Laws are their next attempt at achieving control. Mass killings are the fuel to push it through.

With all this talk about Red Flag Laws, gun-buybacks, and gun confiscations, there's one thing that gun-owners often don't recognize about the anti-gun crowd.

Gun-owners consistently bring up the logical argument that, the anti-gun crowd works hard to take guns away from law-abiding citizens but does nothing to get guns out of the hands of criminals. This argument is valid because it's true. Although the Gun-Grabbers claim to want to keep guns out of the hands of criminals, they really want to take guns away from everyone. Some would argue, "more so," from law-abiding citizens because they are typically Republican voters, and the political opposition of the gun-grabbing Left.

However, most Anti-Gunners oppose gun ownership, because they are simply scared of guns. They typically have no experience with guns and they often make no attempt to educate themselves by going to the range or discussing the topic with gun-owners. This lack of knowledge, coupled with colorful anti-gun rhetoric and propaganda from a dishonest media, keeps them in a perpetual state of gun-fear.

The topic of guns has been fashioned to be one of many wedges used to divide people politically.

The most disturbing part of the gun-grab and those who support it is that they typically support banning guns altogether because they have been taught to believe that guns are the culprit. They believe that guns "cause" people to do bad things. They believe that when people have access to guns they often act irrationally. In other words, *the gun made me do it.*" This type of belief is commonly found among those of the victim-mindset, and often among those who feel emotionally-reactive to the outside world.

Fearful Anti-Gunners want nothing more than for guns to just go away. They don't trust you with guns because they wouldn't trust themselves with guns. In this society, who should we be more concerned with; the law-abiding citizen who has never been in trouble, or the fearful Anti-Gunner who believes that guns cause people to act irrationally?

Gun-Grabbers consistently make the "what if" argument *"What if someone gets angry in traffic." "What if two people have an argument?"* They often imply that under these situations and others like them, people will pull out a gun and shoot someone. What they fail to recognize is that, those thoughts are occurring in their own mind. They often don't consider the fact that rational people are able to restrain themselves. Most people look at situations like this and can't imagine someone being so angry that they would want to kill another person, because the thought would never cross their mind. On the other hand, many among the anti-gun crowd can't imagine someone *not* pulling a gun out and killing people when under stressful situations. What does this say about them?

Sigmund Freud coined the term "Projection." In short, Projection is the process of person "A" blaming person "B" for the thoughts that are occurring in the mind of person "A."

Anti-Gunners often want guns banned because they are scared to death at how *they* would react in the presence of a gun.

6. GUN-CONTROL GANGSTERS

Group-Think destroys the free-will of the individual.

Isn't that really the goal of a gang? You know, remove the person's individuality and replace it with a sense of collective-minded thought with a collective-minded agenda. Why do people join gangs anyway? Why do people join radical politically-motivated groups like Antifa? Typically, when someone joins a gang, they are seeking something. What is it? Strength, power, family, a sense of belonging?

What is it, the person may be lacking (or believe they are lacking) if they are seeking out these things? No, this is not a trick question. If someone is seeking strength, they most likely lack a sense of strength in their own life. If someone is seeking power, they most likely feel powerless in their own life. If someone is seeking family or a sense of belonging, they most likely feel alone or abandoned. These are all very common human traits that most of us have probably felt to some degree at one time or another. But what is the difference between someone who can find that strength within himself or herself and someone who needs outside reinforcement so badly that they are willing to give up their own individuality and their own identity to get a sense of it? Yes, I said *Individuality*. You see it all the time from radical leftists. *"But wait, people on the left are the most individual of all!"* Oh sure, they may dye their hair purple and green, pierce their eyelids, implant devil horns under their skin, tattoo their face and fork their tongue to appear unique and express their own individuality, but are they really expressing individuality?

Some may argue that taking those radical steps to stand out in a crowd may be an attempt at convincing oneself that they *are* unique and special. So, why the need to take it to such an extreme? Because it looks good? Or is there some other reason? Sometimes, the first person we need to convince, when we are unsure of something, is ourselves. But how? Let's say for a minute, you feel like one of the crowd, your voice never seems to be heard. You have always lacked confidence. How could you fix that? Well, you could explore the internal thought-process and beliefs that underlie those feelings or you could put on the most dramatic presentation of personal appearance you can think of and display it in public. I'm not saying everyone with a forked tongue is a bad person, but when it's done to create the illusion of individuality by masking the person's own insecurity, it's done for the wrong reason. In other words:

"Before I can convince you that I am a confident individual, I must first convince myself. How could I possibly be an insecure person lost in the crowd with a deep lack of confidence if I look like this? I mean, LOOK AT ME! Who would do this to themselves if they weren't totally different and independent from everyone else?"

The answer: Someone who is desperately trying to convince themselves of something while hopefully convincing the rest of the world. Or, it's creative expression for the "art" of it.

So if you do feel like just one in the crowd and your voice never seems to be heard, where could you go where your unique brand is welcomed and accepted? Where could you go where you can express your own individuality? Somewhere where the people defend minority groups from those vicious and hateful traditional Americans. Somewhere where you can be anything you want to be, regardless of science or reality. Heck, you can be a girl today and a boy tomorrow. Whatever.

Wouldn't it be great if there was a group that would defend all those people who don't feel like they fit in? Wouldn't it be great if there was a group that would fight for the rights of all those people who feel betrayed by society? Wouldn't it be great if there was a group that created a *safe* environment for those people who (have been taught to) feel persecuted because they are different? Wouldn't it be great if there was a group that defended all the victims of society? Well, there is. It's over there on the left side of the American political spectrum. It's a place where you can be whomever you choose. It's a place where everyone agrees because somehow individuality can be found within a group that demands all its members think alike. If they don't, they will be shunned and publically ridiculed. Kanye West experienced this type of ousting when many of his peers publically reprimanded him for encouraging "free thought" in 2018. It was unfortunate for Kanye that his "free thought" was a little too free and didn't line up with the leftist gang of thought police.

This Utopian place where "individuals" are told their voices will be heard while their voices are simultaneously controlled and structured to fit the group narrative is a hoax and a way of giving people what they think they need while using them to push a political agenda.

So what happens when people start to recognize the tactics and strategies of the left and begin questioning their beliefs about the ideals they have been programmed to support? What happens when people start to feel like they are no longer being betrayed by society and want to strive for real independence? What happens when people start to stray from the anti-gun narrative for instance?

They are reeled back in through scary anti-gun propaganda and depictions of gun-owners recklessly putting them in danger in support of this crazy "2nd Amendment Freedom thing."

I have seen anti-gun groups rally in big numbers while spewing hatred, fake statistics and disgusting propaganda. I've also seen anti-American socialist groups rally and trash city parks and gathering places while spreading hate and destruction. The anti-gun events usually happen right after a shooting of some sort. I say "some sort" because it is always the "sort" that they twist to fit their agenda rather than the type of killings that clearly reflect poorly on failed liberal policies. The anti-American rallies usually occur after American values win in the public forum. For example, when a President who says he will secure our borders to protect American Citizens wins an election, the anti-Americans go nuts.

Why is it that *pro-gun* rallies don't bring the same enthusiasm and numbers that anti-gun rallies bring? The Anti-Gunners would love for you to believe that pro-gunners just don't have the numbers in their favor. They and their lap-dog media try very hard to make the public believe that the anti-gun mindset is without a doubt the way the majority of Americans think. But is it true, or is it a façade?

Let's assume that because there are somewhere between 310,000,000 and 660,000,000 guns in America and somewhere between 100,000,000 and 200,000,000 gun owners, that the numbers may actually be in favor of those who support the 2nd Amendment. I call them *real* Americans. In other words, despite the anti-gun media narrative, it is quite safe to say that, of the 325,700,000 Americans (2017), gun-owners could possibly make up the majority of our society. Oh, they're not gonna' like that one. Let's watch the left squirm. Here's how I can back up that claim.

Pew Research Center did a study that showed 30% of adults currently own a gun and half of those who don't say they could see themselves owning a gun. Most anti-gun media sources will reluctantly agree with that statistic as well. Here's where it gets interesting. Keep in mind, these 97,800,000 gun-owners (30% of society) do not account for the people who lied on the survey to keep their gun-ownership secret and it does not account for the illegally owned guns in America. How many gun-owners surveyed decided it is nobody's damn business? 10%? 20%? If you got a call from a stranger, asking you if you own guns, what would you tell them?

Now throw in the guns and gun owners no one knows about. That's a lot of guns and a lot of gun-owners. Why do I bring up this statistic? To help illustrate just how misleading the anti-gun propaganda sources can be when they display anti-gun rallies as gigantic portions of the population in an attempt to dishearten American gun-owners and people who support our 2nd Amendment. Their attempt to paint anti-gun Americans as a majority of people valiantly fighting against a small number of reckless, deplorable clingers falls flat when we look at gun-ownership through a window of reality. The reality is, most Americans own guns and support or 2nd Amendment.

So, what really causes someone to gravitate toward that gang or tribal mentality within the "gun-control" debate? It is the promise of a sense of individuality through a vehicle of conformity. When you watch the anti-gun radical groups spread their hate for traditional America through violent protests in the streets, you not only recognize the hypocrisy in their "violence to stop violence" approach but you can't help noticing their attempts at expressing their own individuality. This ragtag bunch of "individuals" are fighting for government enforced laws and restrictions, they are influenced by a media that manipulates them and they are convinced that they are doing the right thing. Did you catch that? People calling themselves "individuals" while protesting against freedom and calling for more government control.

So, why is it so easy to get those of the liberal-progressive persuasion to gather while getting gun-owners to collect in support of a cause is sometimes like herding cats? It comes primarily from the mindset of those on the left needing to be part of a larger group as we talked about in the Anti-Gun Cultism chapter. The security in numbers is important to those who want power and need to feel safe. Conservatives on the other hand don't often need that sense of group association because there is a strong sense of rugged individualism among those on the right. It's why Conservatives fight so hard to preserve freedom but don't always feel the need to gather in groups to protest. Assuming that is true, and if you wanted to brainwash someone, it would make much more sense to appeal to a personality type that would be more likely to accept a group-mentality. People who like to be controlled will gather together and recruit other like-minded folks. There is a sense of unity, comfort and safety in the Democrat party. This unity is very similar to the unity found in cults. The problem is that the messaging is often dishonest, always misguided and preys on the reactive emotions of those who find it difficult to view concepts through alternative perspectives.

After reading an article that praised the efforts of radical anti-gun activist Shannon Watts and her attempt to leverage the irrational gun-fear of Levis' executives, it was clear that Watts' focus was severely misguided. To the anti-gun crowd, violating the rights of their fellow citizens is "success," regardless of the number of people left unarmed and helpless in the wake of their "feel good" crusade.

Shannon Watts, founder of the infamous, radical, anti-2nd Amendment group Moms Demand Action for Gun Safety said:

"I think I am living proof that someone who has no experience as an activist can make a difference – I was just a really angry mom of five living in Indiana when I got off the sidelines."

"If you're passionate about an issue and you just keep showing up (and you convince people to join you along the way), you will force change."
– from Levi Strauss website.

Emotionally-reactive activism is usually the motivation used when trying to convince people to join a dishonest cause. If the activists were truthful, they wouldn't get very far, so fear and anger are the tools of choice. Watts even admits that anger was her motivator when she said, *"I was just a really angry mom..."* Misguided fear and anger is the fuel that gives people political-license to violate the rights of others; in this case, under the guise of "gun-safety" fueled by "anger."

If the rights of Americans were important to angry gun-grabbers, their mission would crumble very quickly, but because the emotional element that surrounds the gun conversation is so strong (and continually perpetuated by those who benefit from it), the anti-gun crowd will use it to their advantage and never talk about "rights." By perpetuating irrational gun-fear and conditioning society with terms like "gun-violence," "assault weapon," and "weapons of war," the Anti-2nd Amendment Radicals have the advantage of fear on their side. They can manipulate non gun-owners into believing that guns *cause* violence. In other words, *"if the killer didn't have access to a gun, he wouldn't kill."* The Anti-2nd Amendment Radicals can also train people who aren't paying attention, to believe that gun owners are recklessly and intentionally putting everyone in danger. This builds hatred toward gun owners. They say things like, *"the blood is on your hands,"* when trying to place the blame for a murderous madman's actions on their fellow Americans, Tellingly, these hypocrites often direct this vile, vitriol toward women who simply want a gun for self-defense. It clearly shows their priority is "no guns," no matter how much the other side of their mouths say "Me Too.")

"The blood is on your hands," is a way of shaming people into supporting the gun-grab. This could be the most deceitful and dishonest tool the anti-gun crowd uses because it pushes people, who don't have all the information into a corner and forces them to get on board or suffer the consequences of being a public outcast. The Anti-2nd Amendment Radicals know exactly what they are doing with this terrible accusation and they don't care.

Logical, thinking people scratch their heads and wonder how it is that everyone doesn't question the Anti-Gun Radicals about the fact that their focus is on "gun-violence" when it should be on "human-violence." The anger is directed at the NRA and good folks who want to protect their families, when it should be on those who support Gun Free School Zones, then exploit the death of children to push for more gun-restrictions. If everyone denounced the manipulative anti-gun propaganda and demanded that the focus be put on the actual causes of "human-violence," the spotlight would be on all the things the anti-gun, political-left supports; open borders, sanctuary cities, rampant pharmaceutical drug use, welfare dependency, and Gun Free Zones.

Can't have that, can we?

Nope. It's gotta' be about guns.

The most effective tool the Anti-Gunners have is the power of perception. If they can re-direct your focus, they can sway public opinion. They do this through the use of terminology like "gun-violence," "weapons of war," "assault weapon," and many other terms that evoke an irrational fear of guns. Along with terminology, the anti-gun crowd will use "statistics" calculated in studies that are done for the purpose of proving a biased anti-gun result. Often times the "studies" are conducted using anti-gun lobbying money, then reported on in left-wing publications, followed up by "fact-checking" conducted by left-wing biased groups like Snopes.

Once the base data is constructed and made public, groups like Moms Demand Action and Everytown for Gun Safety, peddle the faulty information to any and every media outlet that will regurgitate it. The narrative that makes its way into your living room on the evening news can be very convincing if you're not paying close attention. It is designed to create fear in the hearts of people who don't know any better, while urging them to support more gun restrictions.

The message is always the same. "We must do something." That "something" is always implied to be more gun-restrictions, even though we have thousands of gun-restrictions on the books that have proven to be ineffective at stopping human-violence. What if the anti-gun smokescreen is really a cover-up for a much more nefarious culprit?

In an article by Dan Roberts for Natural News, Dan talks about pharmaceutical drug use often being directly linked to shootings and how mind-altering medications can convince traumatized youth to harm themselves and others.

"... all of the perpetrators were either actively taking powerful psychotropic drugs or had been at some point in the immediate past before they committed their crimes," wrote Dan Roberts in an article for *Ammoland.com*, which was reposted to *Natural News*.

A list provided by the Los Angeles Times of the shooters it looked at clearly reveals that almost every single one was taking Prozac, Paxil, Zoloft, Luvox, Effexor, Xanax, Ambien, Lexapro, trazodone, and/or some other similar mood- and mind-altering drug right around the time when they flipped a switch and went on shooting sprees. This according to Natural News.

"Those focusing on further firearms bans or magazine restrictions are clearly focusing on the wrong issue and asking the wrong questions, either as a deliberate attempt to hide these links, or out of complete and utter ignorance," Roberts contends.

So why do the Anti-2nd Amendment Radicals refuse to talk about this? Could it be, they profit monetarily from their anti-gun position? Could it be they really do want a gun-free society for the Utopia they think it will bring? Could it be they really are ignorant to the truth. Or could it be, they would be embarrassed to admit that they have gotten it wrong the entire time?

Regardless of their motivation, which could be a combination of all those, they have a responsibility to the families who lost loved-ones in these avoidable mass-killings.

While the Anti-2nd Amendment Radicals perpetuate the gun-lie, ignore the real causes of human-violence and work hard to disarm law-abiding citizens, lives are lost. The question is, are the gun-grabbers in any way responsible for these deaths? The anti-gun media and the dishonest lobbying groups have a responsibility to tell the truth. In the meantime, it is the responsibility of those who see through the lies, to hold them accountable.

The dangerous push to disarm Americans is a clear example of deceitful people misleading others who don't know any better by leveraging their own fear and anger against them. If people were able to see how the anti-gun propaganda is designed to mislead them, anti-gun groups would be seen for what they really are,

"Fearful, angry Anti-Gunners chasing a ghost that never existed, while simultaneously putting good people in danger to support a political agenda."

Luckily for the anti-gun groups, some people would rather be led by reactive-emotion than logical-thought. Here are some facts for those who want the truth.

- *Gun Free Zones have been the target of more than 98% of all mass shootings – Crime Prevention Research Center. (Anti-Gun Groups support GFZ's)*

- *Guns are used 2.46 million time per year in America to save lives – Centers for Disease Control (report was hidden from the public for 20 years)*

- *90% of criminals surveyed in jail, admitted to avoiding background checks when acquiring firearms – Department of Justice study.*

There is no such thing as "gun-violence," only "human-violence." Unfortunately, Anti-Gun Activists are obsessed with guns and refuse to talk about the real problems. They desperately need to recruit more gang-members who are willing to blindly follow their mission and fight relentlessly against those whom they've been taught to believe are the enemy. You.

As part of their mission to misrepresent guns in America, they have developed yet another strategy. You have to admit, they are clever. In yet another attempt to discredit lawful gun-ownership, radical anti-rights groups like Moms Demand Action, have re-defined "The Gun Free Zone" because apparently, you had it wrong this whole time. First, lets look into the minds of the anti-gun crowd so we can understand their madness.

In an article by Meg Kelly – Video Editor for "The Fact Checker," published in the Washington Post, Kelly made the following claim: ***"gun-free zone" is subject to interpretation.*** Kelly's claim is based on the notion that because Moms Demand Action has fabricated their own definition of "Gun Free Zone," the term is now indiscernible. This is convenient for the anti-gun crowd because it muddies the waters and makes the measurement of "gun-free zone death" data nearly impossible.

Moms Demand Action "Gun Free Zone" Definition is as follows: *"Areas where civilians are prohibited from* *carrying firearms and there is **not** a regular armed law enforcement presence."*

Well, this changes everything. At least in their minds and among those who aren't paying attention. So, it looks like, based on the "new" definition, we are supposed to eliminate places like Sandy Hook, Parkland and others when trying to measure the death and destruction that occurs in areas where people are prohibited from defending themselves with a firearm. According to the leftist gun-grabbers, there's nothing to see here because as long as there was a security guard on duty or law-enforcement in the vicinity, it was not a Gun Free Zone.

Do we all remember Scot Peterson, the Sheriff's Deputy at Marjory Stoneman Douglas High School, who ran and hid while students were being massacred? Don't forget, civilians were prohibited from having guns on campus, leaving the safety of the students in the hands of Peterson, but because he was armed, and according to the new left-wing definition of GFZ, Parkland shouldn't be counted as a GFZ. Keep in mind, according the Anti-Gun Radicals, as long as a 500,000 square foot school has one armed security guard, even while prohibiting teachers, staff and lawful gun-owners from carrying a gun, it should not be considered a Gun Free Zone.

The anti-gun mob doesn't want the "Gun Free Zone" being blamed for mass-killings because they support them. The creation of Gun Free Zones are a political win for the left and another road block for lawful gun-owners. This is why the political left cheer in the streets when Walmart declares it's stores gun-free. Should the public become wise to the dangers of the GFZ, the Anti-Gun Radicals would have to admit that they share responsibility for the loss of innocent lives. Denying the dangers of GFZs has become impossible, so rather than admit they support these "Killing Zones," they attempt to change the definition so you can't measure the data. They desperately scrub the blood off their hands, while simultaneously using school killings to support gun-control legislation. Yes, they want it both ways.

Kelly even said in her 2018 article: *"Without a commonly accepted and uniform definition of "mass shooting" or agreement on what constitutes a "gun-free zone," it's difficult to settle this debate."*

Of course it is. That's the idea. The numbers show us that GFZs are deadly killing zones because the people are sitting ducks and the Bad Guys have zero opposition, but the gun-grabbers want desperately for that truth to be clouded in a dispute over the definition.

Regardless of the left's interpretation, the 1990 Gun Free School Zones Law, had a provision for schools to authorize designated people to carry a gun on campus. So let's be clear. Just because an armed security guard is on the premises, does not disqualify the area as a GFZ. There should be no dispute about the definition of a Gun Free Zone. A Gun Free Zone is any area where citizens are prohibited from carrying a firearm.

Based on reported accounts in a study conducted by Gary Kleck and backed by CDC data, there are approximately 2.46 million defensive gun uses in America per year. In other words: "lives saved because of guns." These are specific cases where the presence of a gun stopped or deterred a threat.

The anti-gun left desperately clings to the claim that armed citizens do not stop mass-killings. How do they measure something that hasn't occurred? When the anti-gun crowd tries to claim armed citizens do not stop killers, they are trying to use a hypothetical argument as data. Unlike the Kleck study, the claim that "armed citizens do not stop mass-killings" is impossible to measure because the "killing" they are referring to never happened and the "armed citizen" they are referring to never existed. The entire scenario they are creating, never occurred, therefore it is impossible to measure.

By changing the definition of Gun Free Zone, the anti-gun crowd is able to avoid responsibility for putting children in danger while continuing to portray themselves as virtuous.

Good Gun Bad Guy 3

7. LIBERAL LEVERAGE

Violence is encouraged by some because it locks in support by leveraging a person's bad behavior against them.

How is it that Anti-Gunners, who may otherwise seem to be logical thinkers be so easily influenced to go against logic and reason in favor of reactive, emotional fear-campaigning? To answer that question, we first need to recognize that the people who fall prey to the anti-gun fear-campaign are typically the same people who subscribe to *all* the causes that are served up on the left. All the liberal-progressive causes are packaged together. You can't pick and choose your beliefs. They are chosen for you and come in a bulk package with a bunch of other ideological goodies and guidelines. So if you get tired of protesting one particular "national-injustice," or if that particular "rage-of-the-week" runs out of favor, you can easily be directed by the media to jump on a different one. Chances are, the protest signs have already been printed up and are waiting for you pick them up.

This organized, ideological herding serves a purpose but its participants never seem to reap any of the rewards. It's kind of like summer camp for radicals, but there's a catch. If you are going to sit at the liberal popular table you must eat from their menu and their menu only. In other words; *"If you want to hang with the cool kids, don't you dare show any support for traditional American values."* The good news is, as I write this, the left-wing popular table is being held together with scotch tape and bubblegum and the only thing left on the menu is moldy toast, three day old tofu sausage and a bowl full of day-old hate. However, there are still some diehard anti-Americans pushing the two-for-one breakfast special and there are still many weak-minded, directionless people looking for something to eat and someone to tell them what to think. So in other words, there will always be a table on the left. The question is; how popular will it be and how badly will you have to abandon your morals and common sense to qualify for a seat?

There are a few strategies put in place to convince people on the left to stay on the left. First, as I stated, there must be a place to go. If not a physical place; a metaphorical place. This is why they have created a popular table within their environmental bubble. The "popular table" is where they feel welcomed and praised. Remember, the popular table appeals to those who need reassurance. It attracts people who can't stand on their own when defending their personal or political beliefs and gives them a sense of community and strength. By getting an invitation to the popular table, the person may feel a sense of validation and support from others within the group. The downside of sitting at the popular table is you must never stray from the ideals (rules) presented there. If you do, you will be shunned, punished and ridiculed. This is the leverage that is wielded at the popular table.

To some, being excluded from the group is devastating so they will conform and take on the beliefs that others at the popular table have embraced. Some will naturally gravitate toward the popular table because they inherently love what's on the menu and others will beg to be accepted at the popular table, by abandoning anything that may appear conservative or "traditional-America," (even their own family and God) because they desperately seek the validation that they believe they will receive. In exchange for acceptance and validation, they will soon give up the right to their own thought and free speech but they don't care as long as they feel like they are on the winning team. This can be seen at almost any university in America. Students will jump on board and fall in line with the liberal-progressive agenda regardless of their true values. This will be encouraged by their peers and often leveraged through biased grading from their professors. If they don't completely change their personal beliefs to conform to the rules of the left, they must keep quiet and never reveal them in public, or suffer the consequence of peer-pressure and discrimination. This doesn't only happen at schools. Adults will play this childish game with each other as well. Don't believe me? Ask any left-wing Jewish person how they were able to support Barack Obama's disregard for Israel and support of radical Islam over their own religious beliefs and country of origin. Ask your Jewish Democrat friends why they continue to support freshman congresswoman Ilhan Omar after her repeated anti-Semitic remarks. In the hierarchy of things, Democrats put politics at the top of the ideological food-chain; even above religion. That's why it is so easy for them to abandon their religious beliefs in support of the daily slop being served up at the popular table.

On the left, politics is the new religion.

Another strategy that is implemented to retain left-wing loyalty is the belief that their opposition is evil. People on the left may denounce religion because somehow believing in God is foolish and taking a purely scientific approach to life makes them much smarter and more evolved than others. An example of this would be in the way they call an unborn baby, a "non-viable clump of cells." They will often announce their atheistic views publicly, but if you notice, they do still believe in the Devil, which happens to be a religious figure. This is convenient for them because although their team teaches them that they are much too smart to worship God, they need the Devil in their narrative because the Devil represents evil. They love accusing their opposition of being evil. Without painting traditional-Americans as evil, they can't build the contrast they need, to portray themselves as virtuous. Along with the "evil" label comes an inherent hatred. Once they convince themselves that Conservatives, Republicans and traditional-Americans are evil they can then justify their hatred for them and encourage others to join in the delusional fun. Violence soon becomes justified, because, remember, they are the good guys saving the world.

The interesting thing about the radical left's hatred is that it was already there. They have owned it forever. They just need someone else to blame it on. The last thing radical-anti-American leftists want is to be accused of being evil themselves because they have put a lot of effort into building a virtuous and caring public persona. You know, they care so much about giving those poor sanctuary criminals a safe environment and forget about the law-abiding legal citizens that have to live in fear on a daily basis because of their politically-biased decisions. Ironically, the American citizens living in these criminal safe-spaces are typically unarmed and helpless due to the laws that these liberal activist politicians put in place. So although the idea of evil-incarnate contradicts their religious views, they will use the concept to their advantage when talking about Conservatives and hope no one sees their hypocrisy. Those on the left who hold their religious views in the *highest* esteem, tend to be much less politically active. It's difficult to support abortion while simultaneously embracing the sanctity of life and going to church on Sunday. It's easy, however to support abortion and the disarmament of your fellow citizens after you have denounced God and begun praying at the altar of science and politics.

Punishment is also a very effective motivator, which is why a common practice on the left is to ridicule, demean, and punish others that disagree with their worldview. Liberal-Progressives know, that should they stray from the left-wing menu, they too will be a victim of that same treatment. They will be shunned, punished, and ridiculed for going against their party's ideology. This leverage against them is very strong. Punishment is a strategy they use with an inherent fear, because they know that the very same consequences they place on their peers may one day be used on them. If the leverage of punishment should prove not strong enough, they will be reminded that there is always the leverage of the legal system. These people live and die by the legal system, which is why conservative judges are so scary to them.

Often times, encouraging people to do destructive or even violent things is effective because once the crime is committed, those who committed the act are shackled by the much needed support of their party. An example of a Democratic politician inciting violence is when Democrat Congresswoman Maxine Waters publically called for Democrats to take aggressive action against President Trump and his administration. She said,

"Let's make sure we show up, wherever we have to show up and if you see anybody from that cabinet in a restaurant, in a department store, at a gasoline station, you get out and you create a crowd and you push back on them and you tell them they're not welcome anymore, anywhere!"

Why would Congresswoman Waters want to put her supporters in such a dangerous and potentially illegal situation? Could it be that once people commit a crime, they lose their lawful integrity and become easy to manipulate? Should Democrat supporters cross the party they have professed allegiance to, they become vulnerable, without leverage and at the mercy of their party because they now need the support of the group. We saw this with Jussie Smollett in 2019. Jussie created an outlandish fantasy where he was supposedly attacked by Trump supporters. He went on left-wing media shows to share his traumatic story with the world and gained great support by his fellow, political peers. It was only when his story became so unbelievable that even his Republican hating friends couldn't support him anymore. They soon dumped him like a sack of rotten tomatoes when they realized that they were starting to be tarnished with his bad reputation as they continued to support him. Remember, public persona is more important than loyalty at the popular table and when Jussie was indicted, all his "friends" deleted his number from their contact list.

While you're in the good graces of the political elite, it is important to show your allegiance by making a stand against the "Oppressors." Often this will include breaking the law, but it's ok, if it's for a cause the political left supports. By convincing people to commit crimes or acts of verbal abuse against the opposition, the instigator also puts himself in a position where it's hard for him to turn back -- because if he did, he would have to admit that the actions (often vile) that have been committed against the opposition, were wrong. The peer-pressure strategies of the left are not used on Conservatives nearly as much as they are used on Liberals. Typically because Conservatives will never fall in line with liberal strategies and also because the efforts are much better spent on people who are already willing to blindly support the team. Unfortunately, it is often too late by the time people realize they have been taken for a ride on the progressive crazy train. At which point, liberals will either abandon their party or go the other way and completely commit themselves to the cause.

Here are some examples of people going too far with their rhetoric and destroying their own reputations by calling for violence against President Trump and Republicans:

- *"I have thought an awful lot about blowing up the White House."* -Madonna
- *"I'd Like to Punch Him in the Face"* -Robert De Niro
- *"Pick Up a G*ddamn Brick" if Trump Fires Robert Mueller - David Simon*
- *Actress Lea DeLaria Threatens to 'Take Out' Republicans and Independents with Baseball Bat after Trump Win*
- *Marilyn Manson Kills 'Trump' in Music Video*
- *Rapper Everlast Warns Trump: "I Will Punch You in Your F*cking Face"*
- *Larry Wilmore Jokes About Suffocating Trump with 'Pillow They Used to Kill Scalia'*

Are these calls for violence and angry rhetoric simply misguided anger or a way of encouraging more violence and normalizing hatred among those easily misled people looking for acceptance among their peers?

The radical left-wing-hate formula is simple.

1. Normalize violence.

2. Encourage supporters to commit violence in support of the cause.

3. Enjoy your new recruits and capitalize on the fact that they have lost good legal standing in the community and are

now committed to your cause based on their need to justify their actions.

If people commit acts of violence in support of a cause, they will more likely become a longtime supporter of that cause because changing their political position would also include accountability for their previous actions. This is why violence is encouraged in some circles. It locks in support by leveraging a person's bad behavior against them.

When the threat of legal leverage is not quite enough, praise helps encourage some. Praise them for the work they do regardless of how destructive it is. As long as the efforts they make, work to undermine the opposition, mountains of praise and adulation will be given. Liberal-Progressives seem to respond very well to the old carrot and the stick strategy. The carrot being praise; the stick being punishment. Leaders at the top have figured this out. Fortunately for them, their supporters have not. This is how groups like Antifa grow. Plus, a little walking around money and hotel rooms from wealthy donors doesn't hurt.

Another way the Left gains leverage is through "minority placement." When the political-right seeks election victory, they look for votes from those who want a traditional America. In exchange they promise those voters that they will uphold traditional American values; a strong economy, gun-rights, religious rights, freedom of speech, a strong military and all the things our Country was founded on. Whether or not they deliver on those promises, is another story. It's different on the left.

When the left needs votes they pander to minority or social-justice groups because they know that if they can generate enough support, they can out-vote traditional Americans. You'll know this is true because around 2011, Democrats abandoned the white, middle class, blue-collar voter in favor of anyone else. Not only did the white, middle class get ignored by Democrat politicians, they got demonized. Racist! White Privilege! Bigot! ...etc.

In modern times, minority groups are not only defined by color or race. Minority groups have been created based on social values as well; Climate-Activists, Socialists, abortion supporters, Anti-Gunners, multiple genders, and the list goes on. The goal, for the Left, is to capture as many people as possible by appealing to as many individual, emotionally-driven causes as possible. That may be why they have added so many letters to the gay community? LGBTQ... More identities, equals more potentially displaced members of society. The more groups the left can carve out of the American culture and make feel victimized, the better chance they have of pulling votes from the Republican/Conservative pool because the chance of minority or social group voters with values that overlap the Republican voter block becomes greater as these groups become more plentiful. Whatever happened to the "melting pot?" The Left figured out that more "individual identities" brings more division. Division creates competition. Competition equals votes if they can be given a team to join. Plus, there's a certain level of righteousness in being the victim or oppressed.

What if we could all be "Americans?" ...Sorry, that ship has sailed.

The reason it is possible to pull voters is because most often, the emotional causes trump rational thinking. There is

145

more likelihood that voters can be picked from the Republican pool, if more personal causes can be given a group-identity that the Left can pander to. An example would be, a non-gun-owning Republican. If that non gun-owning Republican can be scared into anti-gunism, the left awaits him with open arms. His gun-fear, regardless of how illogical and fabricated it may be, might outweigh his party loyalty causing him to vote for the politician that promises to keep him safe. On the left however, party loyalty typically holds the highest position of hierarchy.

Don't believe me? Then ask yourself why it is that the left-wing media and politicians are the only ones out there screaming for their causes and demonizing anyone who doesn't agree with them. There is a whole lot of hysteria around climate change, gay rights, abortion, and those scary guns. It's because they have done the math and they know that the more people they can isolate and enrage, the more voters they can pull to their side, as long as they have a corresponding minority group to place them in or protest group they can associate with.

The left's gun-fear campaign has been successful in gathering people who may have never given guns a second thought in the past. There was a time when non-gun-owners weren't scared to death of guns. What changed? Knowing that fear is the strongest human emotion, the left propagates gun related attacks and convinces those who don't know any better that they could be next if they don't get on board with the gun-grab. This is why Democrat politicians will say things like, "We have to get these weapons of war off the streets of our communities." It brings the fear close to home, in the hopes of pulling votes from the Republican pool.

Our Founding Fathers may not have envisioned some of the strategies these enemies of traditional America would use, but they knew the gun-grabbers would be coming. That's why the 2nd Amendment was written. So, although we don't have to worry about Beto O'Rourke physically coming for our guns, we should be very concerned with the ideology of the Left because it is dangerous. Many have lost sight of what this country is all about. Many of them are young enough to have never had real American values to begin with.

Good Gun Bad Guy 3

8. SAFE SPACE

Liberals don't want to control you as much as they want to be controlled.

Broadway and Washington at night – Saratoga Springs, NY

I was stopped at the red light, facing south on Broadway, at the corner of Washington street in my hometown of Saratoga Springs, NY. The sun is shining, the town is alive and it is the middle of track season. Saratoga Springs attracts horse racing enthusiasts from all over the world. To the right of me, on the corner, is a Starbucks and the Latte Crowd quietly and in a very organized way, shuttle in and out without saying a word to each other or anyone around them. Most have much more

149

important things happening on their phones than could ever be occurring in real-life. They generally keep to themselves, as they trade dollars for trendily packaged caffeine and swiftly move on to whatever awaits them.

On the surface, it would seem, these folks are on their way to something very interesting, but underneath their preoccupied scurry there seems to be an avoidance of living in the moment. A disconnect to the reality of life that surrounds them. You'll see this anywhere across the country. Some people are physically here but build an invisible wall around themselves. There is a sense that they are unavailable to communicate at the moment. Almost like the lights are on but no one is home. Sure, they'll exchange the socially required communicative responses. You know, things like, *"I need a Grande, Chai Tea, 3 Pump, Skim Milk, Lite Water, No Foam, Extra Hot, Latte,"* but when it comes to real human interaction and communication, there seems to be a very distinctive disconnect.

Communicating with others is not always easy, I'll admit. There is a certain amount of effort needed to understand the personalities of others and sometimes make accommodations to build rapport with some people when personalities don't line up, but often, out of those interactions, we find that people can teach us a lot and some of the best relationships can develop from some initially uncomfortable encounters. Some people however, just choose not to engage.

Then, there are some people who walk the streets in town, holding hands, talking, petting dogs and looking around at buildings and other things that catch their attention. These people seem to welcome interaction with others. What is the difference between these people and their level of connection with their surroundings? I have always found it amazing that some people enjoy every bit of their life while others seem to be going through the motions and avoid interaction with the real world at all costs. Some will chase you down just to say hello and others will never even know you just held the door open for them.

Usually when we avoid something, it is out of some underlying fear we have for that thing or what that thing represents to us. When we talk about guns and how Anti-Gunners would never think of going to the range, we understand that the avoidance is driven by an incessant fear of guns that has been perpetuated through scary anti-gun propaganda and angry rhetoric. When we look at the avoidance of personal interaction and the constant need to be preoccupied with the digital world, it reveals a different kind of fear.

The fear of reality.

What is the worst part about living in the moment for some people? What could possibly be so horrible about taking in the scenery and saying hello to someone you never met before? What is the worst thing about catching a complete stranger's eye and exchanging a smile? To most people, nothing, but some will do anything they can to avoid it.

Could it be the fear of connection, the fear of self-reflection, or worse, the fear of the responsibility we have for the interactions we engage in? The avoidance of self-reflection is important to recognize and the fact that our digital world keeps us constantly entertained and preoccupied can also give us an excuse to avoid exploring our own thoughts, but the avoidance of people brings another element to the table. Not wanting to engage in society shows that rather than connecting with others and interacting with the world around us, some

151

would just rather disengage and avoid their personal role in the real world. You may call that anti-social.

Yes, I have done it and I'll bet you have too. The question is, do we really want to stay in that perpetual state of isolation? My guess is that we don't but I am concerned that some people may begin to find it way too comfortable being there.

Back to the red light at the corner of Broadway and Washington. As I am waiting for the light to change and while the intersection flows with activity in all directions, I notice something that catches my attention. It's a young woman in her early-to-mid-twenties with her face buried in her phone at the crosswalk. I watch as she takes a quick glance at the "walk" sign and steps off the curb heading east across the busy intersection. With a coffee cup in her left hand and her right thumb typing at top speed, she strolls across the intersection staying on the white painted crosswalk and never taking her eyes off her screen. Not even once. She occasionally misjudges her steps due to the settled indentations in the road caused by traffic wear but she keeps going with her head down, typing, the entire time until she makes her way to the sidewalk at the other side of the four-lane road.

As she made her way across Broadway, other people crossing in the opposite direction parted like the Red Sea to avoid bumping in to her as they recognized she was completely oblivious to anything and everyone around her. Somehow this seemed like acceptable behavior and everyone just went along their way as they accommodated Zoey the Zombie and her blind trek across Broadway.

Now I don't know about you, but when I cross the street, I take a slightly different approach. I don't care if there are fifteen people with bright orange flags waving me across the street. I don't care if lights are flashing and the entire city comes to a complete standstill while the Mayor carries me across the street piggy-back, I am still looking from side to side for any cars, bikes, horses, UFOs or Santa's reindeer before and during the time I cross a busy intersection. I have a sense that it is my responsibility to get myself safely across the street, regardless of the fact that a street sign may tell me it's ok to cross. Why? Because I know that my life is *my* responsibility and no one else's.

In America, we have two very distinctively different ideologies which result in two very different ways of thinking about everything from politics, to guns, to crossing the street.

On the Left, we have people who want more rules, regulations, restrictions, laws and requirements. To them this is a way of achieving a controlled, measured and structured environment. It's also a way of giving up personal responsibility. This feels safe to some people and takes the guesswork out of life. This is the Utopia I told you we would talk about. This government-controlled environment is preferable to them because they believe a controlled, society would be best for everyone. They think it will lead to a safe place for everyone where bad people will no longer exist and everyone will be treated fairly under the watchful camera lenses of a government they put in power. They want to create the landscape and they want everyone to obey the rules and act accordingly. In the process, they get the benefit of giving up personal responsibility while pushing the burdens of society off on to someone else. It's never their fault because someone else is responsible to reinforce the rules. In a society like this, it becomes easy to blame your parents, your professor, your boss or your government. When they can't have these responsibility-free-zones, they create them. They call them safe-spaces.

How does this relate to Zoey the Zombie crossing the street? You see, Zoey is willing to give up her own personal responsibility because the street sign told her she could cross. At that point, she is no longer responsible for herself (in her mind). You are! Or in this case, everyone else at that intersection. She believes, either through complete trust, or ignorance, that she is safe to cross the street because the sign said so. Otherwise, she would at least look both ways. Her safety is now the responsibility of the city because they told her it was safe to walk, or the drivers because the red light told them to stop. Heck, if she has to follow the rules, then you must too. This may come from a rule-bound obedience that is being baked into our society under the guise of safety and equality or it may come from an ideology that is teaching our young people to give up personal responsibility in exchange for a sense of entitlement and the ability to blame others if things don't go the way they want. The possibility of being run over by a car gets completely lost in the self-righteous act of demanding *you* accommodate *them*. Zoey could get hit by a car but *"It's not her fault."*

Does this remind you of the riots which led to people believing they could stop traffic on the highway in support of their ideologically-driven protests? Somehow laying in the street is no longer unsafe if it's for an important cause. If the protestors get run over, they can sue the driver. This makes sense to them because personal responsibility has been completely taken out of the equation. This is why these protestors can stop traffic to protest against the cops, but when they get hit by a car, they call… wait for it…the cops.

You may be asking yourself, how could someone walk across the street at a busy intersection and not be concerned with traffic? It's because they have been taught to give up their personal responsibility and push the burden off onto someone else. It's for the same reason someone can trip over their own two feet while walking down the sidewalk and sue the business that happens to be located at the point they fell and broke their ankle. It's also why we have such an embarrassing, chronically-entitled culture in our country. Somehow, if a job that you like, which pays enough to support an entire family while not requiring you to have any skills is not readily available to you when you want it, *"it's not fair!"* It's never their fault and always someone else's. This is the mentality being created by the American-Left. Is it surprising that a political party which loves control, would create generations of people who love to be controlled?

However, on the Right, we have a different way of thinking. On the right, conservative-minded people generally have the inclination to say, *"Get the hell out of my way. I will do what I want, when I want, where I want and with whom I want. Life is too short to let someone else tell me how to live. I will take responsibility for my failures, hold myself accountable for my mistakes and I will enjoy my own rewards. No one will tell me what to do or how to think. I am free and if you don't like that, you can kiss my ...."*

It is the difference between the desire to live in a controlled environment and the instinctive will to be free. This is why we have an ideological split down the center of America. It's why we do not understand each other. Conservatives can't understand why Liberals not only want to give up their rights, but fight to take the rights of their fellow citizens away from them through legislation. Conservatives can't understand why the Left is constantly waging war on the rest of the country by trying so hard to subvert the Constitution and Bill of Rights and making everyone subservient to government. It would seem that when they can't control society because the Bill of

Rights gets in their way, they still find ways to implement restrictions and regulations that make it difficult to live free. Political-Correctness is an example of restricting people without implementing legislation. Gun-Free Zones are a way of restricting the 2nd Amendment while not "legally" infringing on the right to keep and bear.

Liberal-Progressives can't understand why everyone doesn't want to live in a government controlled, regulated, Utopian bubble and give up their guns. After all, the cops will protect you, right? As for all that money you earn… You should give that to people who don't have any, because somehow they deserve it.

It's pretty clear that a certain number of politicians would love to have control over everything you do on a daily basis. They want to regulate your guns, your money, your cars, the food you eat, how much water you use and what historical information is taught to your kids in school. Then there are the people on the left who fall in line with these regulations. They may be your neighbor, the people you see in the grocery store or even family members. Some will create the rules and some will blindly obey the rules.

So although there *are* those who want to be in control of everyone, it's not *always* the case.

The average Liberal-Progressive not only wants to control you… they too, want to be controlled.

…but in order for them to have their giant safe-space, they need to get you to comply. How can they live their paint-by-numbers life while you're running around with all this freedom and guns and stuff. Their fear of facing the responsibilities of the real-world is so scary to some that they will do whatever they can to make sure your rights are taken away and you are put under the same restrictions and control as them. They know you want freedom but they have already given up theirs and they will do and say anything they can to make sure that you give up yours as well. Why should you be free when they are not? Why do you think they keep talking about the Bill of Rights being antiquated? They also say things like, *"When the 2nd Amendment was written, the only guns that were in existence took ten minutes to load a round, therefore no one needs an AR 15."* This is not an accident. This is to undermine the idea of freedom and make you look un"progressive" for believing that traditional American values are even valid anymore.

So how does this relate to the gun conversation? Anti-gunners truly believe that the only reason to carry a gun is because you're scared for your own life. Why? Because that's what they think in their own minds. That's the thought process that's playing out in their brain. It's not what's happening in the minds of gun owners though.

I often get the question,

"Why do you need to carry a gun, what are you so afraid of?"

I try to explain that Anti-Gunners view carrying a gun as a fearful thing. They think the only reason someone would carry a gun is because they're scared. They think this because that's the only reason *they* would carry a gun. They are projecting their own thoughts and fears onto everyone else. They don't understand that there may be other reasons people carry a gun and it's not out of fear.

Conservatives typically will carry a gun because they're responsible people. We feel a sense of personal responsibility

157

and responsibility for those around us. This is the big difference between Liberal-Progressive and Conservatives. Liberal-Progressives want to push responsibility off onto government or police or someone else, while Conservatives take full responsibility for their own lives. So it can be difficult to answer the question *"why do you carry a gun, what are you so afraid of?"* and actually get them to understand. It's hard to help them grasp the concept that we carry guns or have guns in our home out of a sense of responsibility. Not fear. They have a hard time processing this notion. It's a total and complete lack of communication due to a lack of fundamental understanding. There is no way you can teach someone personal responsibility if they believe someone else is always responsible for them. There is no way to make someone see your point of view unless they have a fundamental understanding of it conceptually already.

The anti-gun left have been taught and conditioned for so long to believe that

- government is responsible or
- their parents are responsible or
- the police are responsible or
- their boss is responsible or
- their professor is responsible

Some can't grab ahold of personal responsibility anymore. This mindset changes the way people function in society at every level and creates a world of blamers and victims; the perfect characteristics needed to qualify for the anti-gun club. Take responsibility away from someone and they will function completely different than they previously had. Raise them from birth to believe that someone else is responsible for their actions and you've just created an entitled monster. The worst part is not that they push responsibility off on to someone else, but rather the fact that because they denounce personal responsibility they now need *more* government intervention, government control and government guidance. These people are being trained to give up personal responsibility and their own identity which is why they like the idea of socialism so much.

The thing that makes these people so angry is the idea that they have put themselves in a cage while *you* are free to do what you want. That infuriates them. The reason they will always double down on government control is because they don't want you to have the one thing that they have already given up. Freedom. But with freedom comes responsibility. Some will put their lives on the line to preserve freedom while others will give it up in a heartbeat because responsibility scares them to death.

When Anti-Gunners are not completely ignoring the fact that we have killers living among us in society, they do recognize dangers. This causes them a sense of helplessness in those moments because they have no way of protecting themselves and they know it. Why do you think the anti-gun elite hire armed security detail? Gun owners are not walking around in fear like Anti-Gunners assume. Anti-Gunners however, *are* walking around in fear (unless they have chosen to deny reality) and they reveal themselves every time they open their mouths. The question is, are we able to recognize their thought-process by the words they use? When they say *"Why do you need a gun, what are you so afraid of?"* they are telling you that they don't believe it's their responsibility to protect themselves and the only reason *they* would carry a gun is out of fear.

When they ask you why you "need" a gun they are telling you that they don't believe they "need" a gun because they are not responsible for their own safety. The word "need" (in this case) is a reflection into their mind about the lack of personal responsibility they have and the burden they put on other people such as government, police or security guards for their own personal safety. They want you to do the same. They want you to think like them.

They create political correctness to shield their fragile feelings and they even have areas where they can hide out from all the mean people who try to make them live in the real world. They do this out of sheer desperation and a lack of ability to face reality. It's a cold harsh world out there but these Snowflakes have created a place to go where they can avoid all that. It's called the "Safe-Space;" a world of never-ending rainbows and strawberry scented puppies they can snuggle while watching West-Wing re-runs. Oh yeah, and Lattes. Lots of Lattes. Non-fat of course.

In the process of creating safe-spaces, the left will create the most deadly of spaces. We've talked about Gun Free Zones and how the Anti-2nd Amendment Radicals are able to convince those who can't think, that these killing zones are good. Here's an example of the GFZ taken to the extreme for what appears to be purely political purposes.

In 1990, Joe Biden introduced A bill called the Gun Free School Zones Act. It was signed into law and made it illegal for law-abiding gun owners to have their firearms on school campuses; ultimately making it easier for killers to do their dirty work, but the law left in a provision that would give the schools the ability to designate specific people to carry guns to protect the children, should they choose. This means, the schools could decide if they wanted some of their staff, including teachers, to be trained and armed. In 2019, New York, Governor Cuomo just took that ability away, making it more likely that our kids will be left unprotected.

Since the Gun Free School Zones Act became law we have seen an increase in school killings. There are more school killings because there are much less defensive measures in place. This is in part because some of our political leaders have made it their mission to demonize guns for political purposes even though we know that guns are used up to 2 1/2 million times per year in America to save lives. That doesn't necessarily mean good guys killing bad guys; that most often means the mere presence of a gun will deter a killer. Gun Free Zones eliminate that possibility.

Many schools have decided that the Gun Free School Zones Act has been a dismal failure and a danger to our kids after watching the number of deaths that occur in these areas and the number of killers these zones attract. Due to the high cost of hired security, some schools have decided to create training programs for teachers and staff who want to be part of the solution to stopping the terrible human-violence we have in our society.

If a child, facing a killer in a classroom, could have the choice of their teacher being armed or helpless, which do you think they would choose?

You may be wondering why in a time like this, Democrat law makers in New York would make it even more difficult for our kids to be protected, especially when we know that killers choose Gun Free Zones 98% of the time.

Mass murderers seek out Gun Free Zones because they know there will be no opposition.

161

More than eight states including Florida are creating training programs specifically designed to address the failed Gun Free School Zones Act because they see how dangerous it has been. Governor Cuomo's new law makes sure that New York does not have that option.

How does it make any sense to bus hundreds of children into buildings across the country, keep them there for eight hours a day, five days a week, remove all forms of defense and then post signs announcing that everyone inside is unarmed and helpless? Well, New York Democrats have gone one step further. Not only have they done exactly that, they have made it law in New York that those teachers and children never have the option of self-defense while in school. New York lawmakers have put in place an iron clad barrier preventing school staff from ever being able to protect themselves and our kids. The protection of our children in New York schools is now the sole responsibility of government or a government approved entity. How did that work out in Parkland, Florida?

We don't believe that our elected officials want children to get killed, but we recognize that their politics are clouding their better judgment and quite possibly putting good people in danger.

9. ENOUGH WITH THE HYSTERICS

The truth about Anti-Gunners is, they don't really want to save lives as much as they want to ban guns.

Are we gun-owners ever successful at arguing facts and statistics against the anti-gun left's irrational, volatile, emotional argument? The answer is, very seldom. The only time we are able to successfully debate their emotional argument with facts is if we can bring them to the table and put their emotional argument aside. That hardly ever happens. You'll notice when watching any Anti-Gunner on cable news they will present an often inaccurate fact that supports their argument but leave out contradicting facts that, if included, would destroy their narrative. Then they use their hand-picked fact and back it up with a combination of filibustering, fear mongering, anger, despair and finally a call to action.

That call-to-action is always in the form of some type of gun-restriction that only affects law-abiding gun-owners. That call-to-action always focuses on more gun laws and never includes ideas to solve the actual cause of killings; human-violence. We see this all the time and we gun-owners continue to battle them in the same old way we always have. We fight them on their battlefield using facts and statistics. We never seem to learn that facts and statistics hardly ever hold up against an emotional argument.

I saw Alex Jones on CNN arguing gun control with Pierce Morgan. This is one of very few times someone defending the

2nd Amendment using the same tactics that the left uses. Alex Jones steamrolled Pierce Morgan with a flurry of facts and emotion. Unfortunately Jones' vitriol was so over the top that the truth he was speaking got lost in the rhetoric. If you listen to what he said in the interview, you'll hear much truth underneath his volume. Unfortunately this argument went to the side of the Anti-2nd Amendment Radical who stayed calm, cool and collected. So what does this mean? Is boisterous emotion a good way to help Anti-Gun Radicals see their ignorance? Does it help us to use facts and statistics? Unfortunately, coming from the pro-gun side of an argument, we already have the deck stacked against us even though we have the facts on our side. It's hard to win with facts and statistics, and even when we do, we typically don't change any minds. This is because the anti-gun left has been indoctrinated with an irrational, reactive, fear of guns and a misdirected anger and hatred toward gun owners that seems to be baked into their psychology. Often, their reactive emotional responses to guns are a bi-product of desperation. Desperation to "do something." Anti-Gunners don't know what to do to solve the problems that cause human-violence so they react irrationally. When desperation sets in, we have two options.

1. **React irrationally and boldly.** This is why we often end up with politicians introducing new gun-restrictions after a killing where a gun was used. It's a knee-jerk reaction because people want to take the easiest and quickest route to "doing something." Most often, this is to please their supporters. It never results in anything productive and always puts more gun-restrictions on good people.

2. **Act strategically and thoughtfully.** This approach is a way of looking at a situation and understanding it before acting. In the case of a murder or mass killing, a strategic approach would look at the causes of the violent behavior and address the causing agent (the killer himself). When illogical anti-gun protestors march in the streets demanding that their fellow citizens rights be taken away and political donors threaten to stop funding politicians, you can see why weak-minded lawmakers don't use rational thought.

So what do we do if we can't win the argument or help them see their gun-ignorance by using these strategies? We need to get under their emotion. We need to undermine their emotional argument by using their own fear and reactive emotion against them.

By helping someone recognize their own emotionally-reactive behavior and putting it on full display we force them to acknowledge it.

"Why are you so emotional over this?"

This acknowledges their emotional argument and causes them to question it, defend it or deny it but either way, it is publicly documented. If they are to admit to being emotional, they will have a rebuttal that is negative towards guns. Something like, *"Of course I'm emotional. I hate seeing innocent people killed by gun-violence."* That's OK. The idea here is to help them acknowledge their emotional-reactiveness and bring it out in the open.

"Are you this emotional about other topics?"

For instance, drunk driving takes twice as many lives as people using guns. This will help them compare other things in their life that they are passionate about and will help them place their gun argument in a hierarchy of values.

"What is your main goal with gun restrictions?"

This usually helps people re-focus on what's important to them with regard to the topic at hand. Their answer will most always be "to save lives." They truly believe that they want to save lives and the emotional argument is key in doing so because, they believe emotions will motivate others to take action.

"Do you realize that it takes a person to pull the trigger?"

Help them see that the gun is not the cause of the violence by asking them this question. Of course we have tried this before and they will instantly go to the tried and true response: *"Yes, but we need to keep guns out of the hands of the mentally disabled,"* or something to that affect. It's OK. We're just trying to help them envision a person's finger actively pulling the trigger. Remember, many of these people are so delusional on this topic of guns that they actually disassociate human involvement in a shooting incident. I know it's hard to believe but this is what we are dealing with. Thanks MEDIA.

"So, at least you can acknowledge that the person is the causing agent and what we are really talking about here is 'human-violence,' right?"

Anytime we use the word "right?" it encourages agreement of the other party involved. Our brains instinctively want to agree so this technique is helpful. You'll see this used frequently and it often becomes a verbal "tick" of those on the left. Nodding your head up and down will help encourage agreement as well.

The emotional anti-gun ploy often stems from childhood. When you see a child acting out it's usually because they know they will get their way. What's the difference between that child and one who doesn't act out? The child who doesn't act out has learned that emotional outbursts don't get them their intended outcome. The argument between fact-based gun owners and emotionally reactive anti-gunners is very similar to a parent who stands her ground against a child who is acting out.

Another component that often comes into play when arguing against an anti-gun agenda-driven person is the belief many have that they are just plain smarter than you. Many on the left come from the mindset that they are somehow of the "intellectually elite." This is usually based on a false premise that because they have extensive schooling they somehow have license to reign educational superiority over everyone else. Many of these people are also emotionally reactive which is why we see safe spaces on university campuses. So we often have to deal with a combination of "intellectual superiority" and "emotional-reactiveness." It's quite a combination.

The easier we make life for these people the more emboldened they become. In this particular situation we may be dealing with a highly educated person who believes that they know everything, who is extremely emotionally reactive and has a propensity to act like a brat if they don't get their way. This is a psychological Molotov cocktail and we are trying to argue against it with facts and data. It never works. Exposing their emotional reactiveness and contrasting it with what *they* claim to be selling (truth and facts) often softens the conversation and may allow for easier dialog. So back to the questions that will help them recognize their emotional argument.

"Children often act out emotionally because they learn that they can get what they want if they kick and scream. Are you purposely acting out, or can you just not help it?"

Radical gun-grabbers want what they want with no regard to the effects of their actions and they will always use the emotional argument to sway public opinion. They don't care that disarming people will cause more deaths by giving killers less opposition, because getting their way feels good to them in the moment and allows them the opportunity to avoid their own flawed thought-process on the topic. Emotion is the one strategy that gets them closer to the goal every time. When we effectively undermine their emotional argument we can get them on the same playing field...sometimes. They always have the filibuster when things get difficult. This is when they just don't stop talking. It is important to help them see that you recognize their need to filibuster being driven by a fear of hearing the truth or a fear of others hearing the truth. It's a way to verbally block a message they don't want getting out.

Supporting Gun-Free Zones helps Anti-Gunners feel like they are saving lives as long as they never have to confront the fact that killers choose GFZs 97% of the time. Often when this bit of truth is presented to an Anti-Gunner, they logically can't argue it, so they go back to their emotional, fear-campaign and say something like, *"Yeah but nobody needs an AR 15."*

The Anti-Gun Argument Formula:

1. **Anti-Gunners will present a "fact," while avoiding all truths that contradict their intended narrative.**

- For example, they will argue that over 30,000 lives are lost because of "Gun-Violence" each year in America and hope that you don't have anything that would prove them wrong. Although it's true that guns are used to take over 30,000 lives per year in America, when all the facts are presented, this narrative completely falls on its face.

- Approximately 60% of those 30,000 deaths are suicides, which in the absence of a gun, would be committed by other means, studies have shown. Anti-Gunners would like you to believe that if guns were banned, people wouldn't kill themselves.

"Well, I was going to kill myself today but I'm not allowed to have a gun, so I guess I'll just make a sandwich and finish folding the laundry."

- After removing the gang-related killings and police-related defensive killings by gun, we are left with approximately 2,500 gun-related homicides. Gang-violence stems from economic and/or societal problems that are often caused by the very people who try to ban guns. The ironic thing about this statistic is that while they create and/or support a depressed environment that produces high levels of gang-violence, they use the homicide statistics against law-abiding gun-owners.

The statistics that result from their bad policies are then used to justify more gun-restrictions, which further produce more killings and increased statistics.

2. Anti-Gunners position themselves as the saviors.

- They want to be seen as the good guys doing everything they can to save lives while positioning gun-owners as the people who are putting the public in danger. In other words, if not for them being there to do the right thing, the world would fall to pieces.

- The truth is, over 10,000 people die per year in America due to drunk-driving related accidents (4x more than gun-related homicides) yet gun-grabbers never seem to find the time to work on that. The gun-grabbers don't want you talking about alcohol related deaths because it shows their hypocrisy. They say they want gun-restrictions because they want to save lives, yet they do nothing to end drunk-driving deaths, which would clearly save more lives. The truth about Anti-Gunners is, they don't really want to save lives as much as they want to ban guns.

3. Anti-Gunners will always give an emotional, fear-inducing argument.

"These are the lives of innocent children who just want to play with their friends and go home to do their homework."

Or something cute like that.

- The emotional argument trumps facts any day of the week and the Anti-Gunners know this. The emotional argument is usually not used on a gun-owner when no one else is around. This strategy is only used when there are other people involved in the conversation or in the case of TV and radio, viewers and listeners. It is an interesting strategy because the Anti-Gunner typically thinks that the Pro-Gunner will bow their head in shame when confronted with the emotional argument because they would fear public demonization. This is a way for the Anti-Gunner to set up the Pro-Gunner to appear heartless if they don't engage the emotional cry-fest. This is a projection on the part of the person using the emotional argument because they know they (themselves) would do the same in a similar situation. In other words, the Anti-Gunner knows that emotions win support over facts. It is the foundation of Liberal-Progressivism.

"You'd better support all the causes they defend or you are an insensitive, racist, sexist, homophobic monster."

The gun grabbing, social justice warrior believes everyone fears public shaming for being insensitive because *they* fear public shaming and they typically can't think out of their own sphere of thought to acknowledge a perspective other than their own. They certainly can't imagine reality being measured by anything other than this emotionally-reactive fantasy world they have been indoctrinated into. It's all a big sham and millions of people fall for it every day. Many, build careers on this very type of political positioning.

- Undermining their thought-projecting nature brings a logical component to the conversation. Asking an Anti-Gunner *"if it would be possible for someone to support saving lives without engaging in an emotionally-driven dialog,"* may help diffuse this conversational tactic. Remember, as long as they can pull you into their world of hysterics, you don't stand a chance. It's like getting lured down a dark ally. Your job is to put their reactive, emotional argument on display for others to see and DON'T PLAY. Their fear of public ridicule is debilitating. Their removal from the popular table is their kryptonite.

4. Anti-Gunners will create anger toward those who would oppose them.

"But these gun-owners would rather protect their guns than these little innocent children and the politicians that support these killings are bought and paid for by the NRA."

- By positioning gun-owners as *baby-killers*, the anti-gun crowd has the opportunity to engage in the most sinister tactic possible. They can demonize a portion of society and encourage others to get onboard with the public shaming. Don't forget, when they accuse gun-owners of putting innocent little babies at risk for their lust of guns, they are talking about half (or more) of the American population. Ironically, many of the gun-grabbers are closet gun-owners themselves. This is where it gets interesting. How could someone demonize others with such heinous lies when they know that their family members, friends, co-workers or *they themselves* fall under the same category? Simple but not easy. They only let you see what they want you to see. It's not easy for them to create a sham public persona, it actually takes a lot of maintenance and when their anti-gun hypocrisy is exposed, they run and hide. This is why open-boarder advocates never seem to be able to answer the question; *"How can you justify open-boarders when you have a fence around your personal property?"* The argument for gun-restrictions brings with it the same hypocrisy; *"How can you advocate for gun-restrictions when you own guns or have armed security protecting you?"* Like with the open-boarder position, Leftists present themselves as the "protectors of the innocent" while using the lie to further their own political agenda. They also hope you never expose their hypocrisy.

5. **Anti-Gunners will always offer a solution to the tragedies they promote.**

"We need to ban assault-weapons and implement stricter background checks."

- Anti-Gunners know that they need to have some kind of "facts" to back up any gun-bans or restrictions they propose, so they use the old faithful "Australian Gun Ban."

- Anti-Gunners love to tell you that since the Australian Gun Ban, murders and suicides went down, Down Under. What they don't want to tell you is that the slight downward trajectory was already in motion prior to the ban. The truth is, the Australian gun ban had no significant impact on murder or suicides whatsoever. However, the ban *did* have a significant impact on sexual assaults. Can you guess whether sexual assaults went up or down after Australian citizens were no longer allowed to have guns to protect themselves? You guessed right. They went up. Funny how the gun-grabbers don't talk about that, especially given their position on female empowerment. Or is that another lie the leftists are living?

It seems that any of the emotionally-driven leftist agendas bring with them the same strategies and inherent hypocrisy.

1. Create an opponent
2. Demonize your opponent
3. Present yourself as the Good Guy
4. Capitalize on emotion
5. Generate fear
6. Generate hate
7. Hide opposing facts
8. Never consider the possible negative effects
9. Offer a solution that fits your agenda

When my friend's daughter was young she kicked and screamed because she wanted a pony, but she paid no regard to the fact that the pony wouldn't fit in the house.

Anti-Gunners want gun-restrictions but they pay no regard to the fact that disarming good people causes more violence because it emboldens killers. They don't care that they put people in danger, as long as they get their way... like a child. They don't really want to solve the problem of human-violence because they can easily blame it on guns.

Take any violent act, trace it back to its origin and you will find the real problem. It's never the gun.

Politicians do their very best to keep this logic hidden. They cover it up with scary gun rhetoric and propaganda because as soon as the voting public understands that there are problems we have not been addressing, they will stop supporting gun-grabs. At some point, people start recognizing violence for what it is; human-behavior caused by any number of psychological defects. At that same point, the argument that guns are the problem, begins to look ridiculous. The struggle we gun-owners have is breaking through the relentless assault on the minds of people that keeps them in an endless, fearful, hysterical state of gun-fear. There is a level of ignorance and a limited level of rational thought necessary to support gun-restrictions…and the hypocrisy is maddening. I'll give you an example of this irrational thought-process.

My friend Amanda Suffecool tells the story of the time she was on a plane and my book Good Gun Bad Guy caused a stir. As the story goes, Amanda was sitting next to a woman who was less inclined to except gun-ownership. In this case; a fearful, irrational, Anti-Gunner. Amanda says the woman sitting next to her saw the cover of Good Gun Bad Guy and asked the flight attendant if she could change seats. Yes, she wanted to change seats because of a picture of a gun on the cover of a book. Apparently the picture of the gun triggered her. In case you're wondering, no I'm not exaggerating. This is a true story.

The woman could not stand the sight of the cover of Good Gun Bad Guy, to the point she had to take some sort of action in response. If you've seen the photo of the beautiful 1911 on the cover, you might be asking yourself how this is even possible. How does this happen? We know these people are trained and conditioned to fear guns, but what happens when it goes so far that they fear a picture of a gun? Remember the story of the boy who got in trouble at school for biting his pop tart into the shape of a gun. Was the teacher really afraid of a gun-shaped pop tart? No, it's a much deeper psychosis than that. The delusion and insanity in the minds of some, has gone so far that it causes them to live a life of irrational fear. That irrational fear causes them to make irresponsible decisions and reactive choices in life.

Animals tend to be very reactive creatures, much more so than humans. Well, rational humans, that is. Ever make a sudden movement and your cat jumps five feet in the air? That is caused by a mechanism within the cat for the purpose of life-preservation. It's part of the mechanical structure of the cat. Although humans have a fight-or-flight mechanism, most of us are able to balance it with logic and reason. The idea that this woman on the plane would have such a reaction to a picture of a gun and make such a scene over it, might surprise a logical thinking person, but remember, gun-fear is a brainwashing that goes deep to the core of the beliefs and thought process of people and it is reinforced on a daily basis. It's relentless penetration into the psyche of weak-minded people short-circuits their logical override.

Obviously the woman on the plane knew that a picture of a gun wasn't a problem. To her, the idea of a gun and what it "means" (in her mind) was the problem. Even though some Anti-Gunners think that guns are dangerous, it's still a stretch to believe that they would think a picture of a gun could come to life and kill someone. So, what happened to her when she saw it? Although she had a mental meltdown and negative reaction to the book, this goes more to the support of a belief than the idea that a photo could cause physical damage. Let me explain.

It would seem that this woman's fear of guns was at a heightened level, but her anti-gun position may have been the prominent driver in her need to change seats on the plane. In order to support an anti-gun position, the Anti-Gunner needs to play the full game. The Anti-Gunner needs to defy and denounce Guns at every level possible. In this case, in order for the woman on the plane to stay true to her anti-gun position, she needed to push back on anything gun-related. By acting so disgusted, that she needed to change seats on the plane, she reinforces her beliefs about guns and justifies her irrational thought-process. She strengthens her delusion by giving it credibility and reassures herself that, yes, in fact she is a true Anti-Gunner and she is morally superior for making a stand. She also confirms the notion (in her mind) that guns are bad. Her obnoxious scene proves it. I mean, who would go through all the trouble of getting the flight attendant involved and inconveniencing others around her if it wasn't fully justified? Answer: a crazy person.

People may argue that radical leftists have been psychologically traumatized over a whole list of causes and as a result, have become emotionally reactive. I would tend to agree, but their passionate commitment to activism is an equal, if not greater, motivator of their childish behavior. The job of an activist is not only to spread a message. Activists commit to their cause with the highest level of emotional commitment possible. How else would it be acceptable to stand in the street and oppose oncoming traffic? Do they not know that they are putting their lives are in danger?

Radical activists often work themselves into such a lather over a topic that they let their emotions overshadow any sense of reality. They denounce reality, even when it has a negative effect on their lives or the lives of others. In the case of the anti-gun woman on the plane, had she not reacted negatively, she may have doubted her own level of commitment to the anti-gun cause. In other words, had she not acted out in response to the book, she may start to believe that guns are acceptable in our society…and we can't have that. This type of

177

radical indoctrination, is dangerous because it trains, otherwise logical thinking people, to believe things that aren't true and act negatively in response to things that don't even exist. In this case, an image of a gun. Living life reactively, limits our ability to experience and enjoy all the great things the world has to offer. It renders us emotionally reactive and limits our view of reality. It also makes us pawns to those who would use us in their mission to further their agenda.

Every time Amanda tells the story of the fearful anti-gun activist on the plane, some people laugh and some people appear to be confused. I believe it is sad that there are people among us who have given up rational thought for fearful, angry activism. If they only knew just how bad the media and the anti-gun lobby have manipulated their thought process, they would rethink their entire lives. The reason they don't admit it is because, if they did, they would have to rethink their entire lives.

10. RULES OF WAR

Trusting Anti-Gunners with firearms legislation is like asking a bank robber to hold your wallet.

The one question I get most often is, *"How do I argue with an Anti-Gunner?"* The first thing I say is, we must first focus on understanding them, otherwise we don't have a chance debating them on the topic of guns.

Often, in support of the anti-gun mission, people will find any way possible to justify their position, but when put on the spot, sometimes they can't... For example, when you ask someone who is vehemently against gun ownership, if they have a gun in their home to protect themselves and their family, most won't answer the question. They often say, "It's none of your business" or they will find a way to change the subject. Why? One of two reasons.

1. They secretly own guns but choose to push the politically-driven anti-gun narrative.

2. They don't want to make themselves a target because they actually don't have an adequate way to protect themselves.

Let's look at both these thought processes. When we unpack the thinking behind the first scenario, it breaks down into two different motives. The first motive is to hide their hypocrisy. This applies to those who secretly own guns but don't want anyone else to know because their politics have

179

driven them into this corner and they fear being seen as a hypocrite by their peers. So, they own guns because they see the value they bring but vote for the politician that promises more gun-restrictions. In this case, their politics are stronger than the moral integrity of standing behind their beliefs. They would much rather be part of the "popular table" than defend gun-ownership. Can you see the hypocrisy?

The second motive is that of those who *do not* have guns in the home. These people don't want to make that announcement publicly because they understand the dangerous position they put themselves and their families in by being unarmed and defenseless. This motive requires a lot of mental gymnastics because although they want to make the announcement publicly, they understand the dangers of letting the Bad Guys know that they are vulnerable. They are in a bit of a conundrum. On one hand, they would love to show the world how they practice what they preach but on the other hand they don't want to make themselves a target. They're fine with Gun Free Zone signs at Elementary Schools, but not their own home. In other words, they speak out against gun ownership because it suits them politically but realize how important guns actually are to defend themselves should the need arise. You would think that if they felt strong about their anti-gun position, they would shout it from the rooftop. Can you see the hypocrisy here?

There are also those who *will* announce publicly that they don't own guns because they truly believe they are protected in other ways. There are three ways these Anti-Gunners justify this position.

1.   The cops will save them.

2.   They can protect themselves.

3.   It will never happen to them.

Let's look at scenario number one **(the cops will save them)**. This mindset is purely delusional given all the police response-time statistics we have.

ASecureLife, a company that has been researching the security industry since 2008, says, *"Response times differ from city to city based on factors like city population, police funding, and available resources in a given region. When it comes to Priority 1 calls (the highest-priority emergencies that usually include life-threatening emergencies or dangerous active crimes) the difference between a five-minute and 10-minute response time can make all the difference."*

They released a study showing the following:

City	Population	Police response time (minutes)
1. San Francisco, CA.	884,363	5.46
2. Houston, TX	2,312,717	5.51
3. Los Angeles, CA	3,999,759	6.1
4. New York City, NY	8,622,698	6.69
5. San Antonio, TX	1,511,946	6.88
6. Austin, TX	950,715	7.15
7. Dallas, TX	1,341,075	8.39
8. Seattle, WA	724,745	9
9. San Jose, CA	1,035,317	9.2
10. Fort Worth, TX	874,168	9.5

What do these Anti-2nd Radicals think will happen? Do they think they can ask a violent attacker, who breaks into their home, to take a seat and wait for the cops to arrive? Maybe they will offer the criminal a snack while they wait. In order to support the argument that civilians shouldn't have guns, the people who use the "cops will save them" claim to justify their anti-gun position need to maintain this position, despite the facts. So when they are asked if they are concerned with the 5-10 minute police response time, they don't have a good answer.

How about scenario number two? **(They can protect themselves)**

I often use the story of my friend who told me, he doesn't need a gun because he has a 9 Iron. We were having what I thought was a serious conversation at the time. Given the fact that I knew he held a strong anti-gun position, I asked him if he had a gun in his home to protect his wife and kids. When he told me (with a straight face) that he believed he could stop any home intruder with his 9 Iron, I realized that he either didn't give this much thought or he had done a very good job of believing his own fairytale. I'm not talking about a stupid person here. This friend of mine is what those of the intellectually-elite would refer to as well-educated. Somehow universities have a fantastic way of disabling the portion of the brain responsible for common-sense. When I tried explaining the 6 foot swing radius of a 9 Iron being insignificant when compared to the speed of a bullet from 15-20 feet away, he told me how *"nobody needs an AR 15"* or something like that.

Lastly, let's consider the belief that many Anti-Gunners hold. **(It will never happen to them).**

This is an interesting position because it requires a great amount of ignorance. To disregard the million plus violent crimes per year in America and hold strong to that notion, it takes a lot of mental-maintenance. Every time a violent act is publicized, these people need to find ways to justify it never happening to them. It is a mindset that is cultivated within the "bubble environment" they live. These people are often those who refuse to believe that they could get hit by a car while crossing the road because they had the right-of-way. Remember Zoey the Zombie from Chapter 8?

This is what they see as their most credible reason for proudly announcing their non-gun owning status. (And I'll reveal the twofer they get out of this in a bit...)

Are you or I going to be in a catastrophic collision today? Lose a home to fire today? Die in our sleep because of a carbon monoxide leak tonight? Obviously, the odds are very much in our favor and we go about our lives making plans for next month, next summer, and beyond. Will we ever have to defend ourselves with a firearm? Thankfully, we probably won't. Heck, most police officers retire without ever having to unholster their pistol, let alone fire it in self-defense.

I don't believe everyone should carry. If carrying isn't your "bag," God bless ya'. It's a personal choice that requires a lot of commitment.

Why would you or I choose that level of commitment in expense, time spent training and getting educated, dressing appropriately for concealed-carry etc when the likelihood of "today being the day" is slim? Well, let me ask you a couple obvious questions: why do we have CO detectors in the house, wear seatbelts, have insurance on our homes, and keep a close eye on the drivers around us? Because if we come to the end of a long life and never had to utilize those things, it was cheap peace of mind. And of course, the converse, bottom-line answer is: should we hit the unlucky lotto tomorrow and are unprepared - the downside is too great.

So is it legit for someone to say he doesn't think it'll happen to him? Definitely. If the antis left it at that- as a personal choice, we'd be on the same page. The "twofer" they get out of pronouncing their "I feel no need" status is the implication that people who do carry see muggers and ISIS lurking around every corner. The antis love to paint us as scared and paranoid.

I wonder if any of them have fire extinguishers or emergency funds should the dryer go on the fritz? Paranoid, no. Prepared, yes.

I want to discuss some of the actual strategies that can be used in a gun debate but let me first explain that any debate can be very uncomfortable, especially if you're not used to it. I will be the first to admit that I never thought I would be talking about gun-rights in this capacity, let alone debating the topic. I will be completely up front with you and tell you that I often need time to collect my thoughts and think things through before I have a solid rebuttal to many of the anti-gun arguments. It's not a bad thing if we don't have a snappy response ready to go. The truth is, our brains all work differently and the way we process information, along with the adrenaline that may be present during a heated conversation affect the way we think and respond to things. I say this because you may think that you can't discuss this topic with effectiveness just because you get tongue-tied or are slow at recalling information. You're not the only one.

So let's take it slow and try to understand what we are trying to achieve when we defend our precious 2nd Amendment. First of all, what does it mean to you? Think about it. Why do you even care? Why is it important that you discuss the topic? If we don't have a good reason to defend something we won't be very good at it. Maybe we have good reasons but we simply aren't clear on them. Are you perfectly clear on why you must defend the 2nd Amendment?

Let's start with that. Why is it important to you to defend your right to keep and bear arms? I know I ask a lot of questions, but I have found it to be the best way for me to pull out the meaning behind anything that I do. If we have a strong "Why," we are unstoppable. If we don't really know or haven't clarified it for ourselves, we often waiver.

I don't want to look back down on earth in 50 or 100 years to find out that I could have prevented my son, grandchildren or great-grandchildren from being victims of an over-ruling Government or an act of violence. I hate the thought that people could let American freedom go to waste because they are too scared to speak their mind and stand up against tyrants with too much power. Even worse, I get nauseous at the thought that some people among us are so easily led to believe things that undermine their own freedom. If I have anything to say about it, I will. Now, while I still have the ability to make change. I want to know that my great grandchildren are not slaves to a ruling class, rather free to enjoy all the benefits life has to offer. I never fought in war but I will do whatever I can to preserve the rights of future generations.

That's my "Why." What is yours?

You can see how understanding *why* you want something can help you. Now let's talk about how to put the slap-down to these anti-gun knuckleheads. We already talked about exposing their reactive-emotion in the last chapter but now let's discuss their Achilles heel. They actually have two. I like to lump Anti-

Gunners in with leftists because for the most part they share the same ideological traits. Not all Leftists are Anti-Gun, but all Anti-Gunners are leftists. They would love for us to identify all the specific minorities and social justice groups within the left separately, as to be fair and specific because there are times that some may not hold all the same beliefs or support all the same causes. I don't give a damn what they want and it is much easier to identify Anti-Gunners and leftists together for the sake of *this* discussion because otherwise, we will get forever bogged down in the intricacies of their ideology if we don't. The strategies I will discuss are specific to the gun-conversation but can easily be applied to any leftist argument.

That's the first lesson. **Don't give a damn about their feelings.** You don't have to be sensitive to their emotions. You have no obligation to make them feel good. They don't deserve your respect during this type of war because the first chance they have to destroy you and take advantage of your good nature, they will strike. As Donald Trump would say, "believe me."

The two weaknesses of the anti-gun crowd are "intelligence" and "morality." Both these weaknesses are bred within the left-wing ideology. They are weaknesses because it is what the left capitalizes on as their strengths. Many on the left need to believe they are superior to everyone else and they claim their superiority through higher-education and the notion that they are of a moral high ground. Both exist only in their minds. "Intellectual Superiority" is touted by the left because they believe that with a college education comes a license to shut down any opposing argument. You will hear them use this as credibility all the time. *"I have a PhD in ..., therefore, I am the authority on this matter and you need to listen to me."* They claim "moral high ground" by positioning themselves as the justice warriors. You'll hear them say things like, *"I am fighting for the people who are victims of 'gun-violence'."*

So how do we deal with that narcissistic attitude? We expose them for their lack of common-sense. When someone thinks they are smarter than you, they typically expect to debate you by throwing facts and statistics at you. The facts and statistics that they work with are always gun related and never related to the actual causes of *human*-violence. Their argument is always with the intent of implementing more gun-restrictions. They enter the conversation with confidence and a belief that you don't stand a chance against their intellect. This is exactly what makes them vulnerable. We are not going to try and outwit them but redirect them onto our playing field. While they are focused on the gun, the data they have memorized and preying on the emotions of those who don't know any better, we want to help them see they are completely off base and should be hyper-focused on violent behavior and its causes rather than the areas in which they exploit. Take them off their game.

I understand you want to appear to be educated on this topic but you're way off base. Surely you don't believe that guns *cause* people to be violent?

You'll get a response like: *"No, but if we can keep guns out of the hands of people who shouldn't possess them we can prevent senseless deaths."*

Again, I am questioning your intelligence because it almost sounds like you actually believe that criminals will obey gun-laws. You don't actually believe that do you? Here, we are almost mocking their argument to make it look completely ridiculous.

Use their name when possible. It catches their attention and causes them to listen to you. It gives you a dominating position in the conversation.

Rick, Listen, intelligent people understand that gun-restrictions do nothing to address the societal issues that actually cause human-violence. I'd like you to stay focused on that if you could. Because what we really want to do is stop violent behavior, correct?

I remember Tony Robbins talking about Neuro Linguistic Programming (NLP) and one very powerful way to get a person's attention is to speak to them in the best way they understand. In other words, some people respond differently based on their most acute senses. Some people are auditory, some are visual and some are kinesthetic. You may ask a kinesthetic person how they "feel" about something, you may ask an auditory person to "listen" when you ask them something, or you may engage a visual person by telling them to "look." This is why you will hear commentators and interviewers say things like, *"Listen, I understand your position on the topic, but...?* So when an Anti-Gunner tries pushing propaganda on you, try something like this:

Look, I thought I was going to have an intelligent conversation but you are getting yourself caught up in propaganda and emotionally reactive rhetoric. Can you please try to stay focused?"

So let me understand this Becky. On one hand we have criminals who want to kill people and on the other hand you're offering a magazine capacity restriction. Do you really expect intelligent people to believe that

someone who is willing to kill in cold blood will not exceed the bullet limit?

This response can be used against most gun-restriction policies. It takes the focus off the gun and puts it on the human behavior while exposing the Anti-Gunner's illogical perspective.

How about when the Anti-Gunner tries to engage you in the infamous "background check" debate?

"Background checks prevent gun-deaths."

That's wrong. You're either misinformed or lying. It's a hypothetical argument. How can you measure something that doesn't happen?

How many lives are saved because of background checks?

They can't answer that question. There is no data. We do have contradicting data that shows more gun-restrictions causing more homicides. When the UK banned handguns in January 1997 their homicide rates rose dramatically, up 45% over the next eight years and only came back down after a large increase in the number of police. – Crime Research Prevention Center.

"Do you support background checks?"

90% of criminals surveyed by the DOJ said they avoid background checks for gun purchases. 95% of background check denials are initially false positives. So what does this mean? This means that background checks do nothing to stop Bad Guys from buying guns while 67,500 good people are denied their 2nd Amendment

right every year and made vulnerable to attacks because they can't protect themselves. How is this good?

(False positives happen for a number of reasons such as, similar names, birthdates, social security numbers, mistakes on applications, etc.)

Questions like this will unwind a self-indulged Anti-Gunner when they start throwing typical talking points at you because it pokes at their "intellectual superiority" and helps you manage the conversation. they truly believe they are smarter than you because that is what they have been taught to believe. We're not being mean here. We're just trying to knock them off their game. Here's another little secret. Notice how all the responses shown, end with a question. Putting them on the receiving end of questions keeps you in control of the debate. Always ask questions when you can. Megyn Kelly got into a debate with a guest on FOX News one day and the guest put her on the receiving end of a question. She simply wouldn't answer and said, *"I'm asking the questions"* because she knows how important that position is.

- **What do you mean?**
- **How did you come to that conclusion?**
- **It sounds like you're making that up. Where did you get that information?**

Ok, this should put a dent in their intellectual superiority and soften them up a bit. Now let's poke at their morality. I know this all seems harsh and even uncomfortable but don't forget, they are waiting for the opportunity to do the same thing to you.

Before I go any further, I want to credit Ben Shapiro for parts of the following strategy. His mind is very sharp and although I have developed many strategies to undermine the anti-gun argument, Ben helped bring to light some extremely useful components. I have built on them so they can be applied to the gun conversation.

Anti-Gunners and left wing activists pride themselves on their moral character. This is where all the social justice warrior identity is hatched. They need their causes so they have something to fight against. Why? It makes them feel good about themselves and gives them credibility among their peers. Without the perception of racism, sexism, white privilege and gun-violence they have no reason to put on their cape and fly around Metropolis. The biggest hoax ever perpetrated on America is the package of "isms" the left creates and sells to those who can't critically think.

NONE of their causes exist at levels anywhere near what they need you to believe and some of them are completely made up out of thin air. The fabricated cause that tugs at the heartstrings of Americans the most, is the "gun-violence" sham. There is no such thing as gun-violence, only human-violence, but they desperately need there to be because fighting against it helps them appear to be "morally superior." A great way to shut down an anti-gun leftist is to use their fake "gun-violence" cause against them and expose their immorality in the process. Here are some ways to do that.

It is important to attack first in a debate with an Anti-Gunner because it sets them off-balance and gives you control of the conversation from the start. This should only be done with someone you know has the intention of destroying you. If you are just having a friendly conversation with someone, rapport building would be useful. The best way to attack their

191

moral character is to expose them as evil and dangerous. Your job, early on, is to show anyone listening the fact that their gun-restrictions and efforts to disarm good people and make them vulnerable to attacks is immoral and they are the type of people that put others in danger. Expose the flaws in their personal character.

"You're immoral because you're willing to put good people in danger just to push your political agenda."

"If your moral compass tells you that it's OK to bus hundreds of children into a building every day, take away all forms of armed security and then post a sign that tells killers that everyone inside is unarmed and helpless, then you should go back and reevaluate your morals."

Quickly let everyone listening that you are the one in the argument that wants to save lives, while exposing your opponent as the one who is putting people in danger. Frame them as the bad-guy.

"Preservation of life is a human right and you're evil for trying to take that away from people."

"Why do you think you have the right to make people vulnerable to attacks?"

"It's immoral to put people in danger and frankly not that intelligent a position."

"Which is a higher value to you, people being able to protect themselves or making them unarmed and helpless so you can push a political agenda?"

Stay focused and don't let them take you down the rabbit hole. They will do this by trying to make you defend allegations or by giving you some bogus anti-gun statistics or putting you on the receiving end of a "gotcha" question. A "gotcha" question will be something like this:

"Because over 30,000 Americans lose their lives to gun-violence every year, how can you be against universal background checks?"

You need to get out from under this question quickly and turn it back on them because it is set up in a way that if you attempt defending it, you are defending something that is not even true. The first part of the question is misleading because the "30,000" includes *all* gun-related deaths. Take out suicides, cop-killings and gang-related deaths by gun and you are left with approximately 2,500 gun-related homicides. A good way to respond would be to question their intelligence on this one.

I thought you were smarter than that and would've done your research. You do know that of that 30,000, only 2,500 are non-gang homicides, right? Are you trying to sell people on the idea that we should turn more people into victims by disarming them? Because that's what gun-restrictions do.

When an Anti-Gunner starts going off on tangents like *"The NRA lobbies for the death of children"* or *"No one needs an assault weapon"* get them back on your agenda. Get them to refocus on the causes of "human-violence." Remember, they are all about the gun. That is what they have been trained to do. They see violence through a lens of gun-fear. They can't help it. You know the violence problem we have is a humanity issue but they are so far gone that they don't even consider that. It's your job to help them refocus. If you can bring them back to reality, ask them some more questions.

Listen, Tom, I know you are having a hard time focusing on the "human-violence" element here. It's a hard topic to grapple with. I'll give you that, but let me ask you something. If there was something we could do to fix the real problem, human-violence, what would it be?

They will probably revert back to some form of gun-restriction argument, but at least you made them think about the real cause for a second, which is "human-violence." Don't be afraid to leave them in silence after you ask a question. Ask the question, then shut up. Avoid the temptation to fill every void with words. We sometimes inherently get uncomfortable when there are breaks of silence in a conversation but in this case it helps you because it leaves them struggling to answer your question and the moment of silence shines a spotlight on their inability to come up with an answer.

When talking with an Anti-Gunner, they want you to be argumentative and irrational. They expect you to say things like, *"No one is gonna take my guns!"* Don't be that guy. Instead, let them have an insignificant win now and then. What I mean is give them little victories. For instance, they will try to trap you when they can and make you look unreasonable. They hope to put you in one of their stereotypical scenarios by asking you questions like:

"Are you against all restrictions on assault weapons?" Although you may not support any restrictions (rightfully so), they want to hear you say it. Don't give it to them. They have created such a fantasy around semi-automatic rifles ("assault rifles") that if they can get you to defend them, somehow they think they can put you in their "crazy gun-owner" category.

You're not going to let them do that but you can give them a little victory by complimenting them to soften them a bit and then go in for the kill. Here's what you do when they ask the question:

"Are you against all restrictions on assault weapons?"

That's a great question. (that's their win. It's not much but they like hearing it. Plus you'll go on to repeat their term "assault weapon." They love that.) **Assault weapons have been defined in many different ways. Some say it has to be fully-automatic, some say semi-automatic. Some have qualified them as assault weapons if they have pistol grips, detachable magazines, muzzle brakes, a bayonet lug, weigh a certain amount or any number of different attachments or accessories. Just so I know what we are talking about, could you give me your specific definition of an "assault weapon?"** Then shut up. It's kinda' fun at this point because they can't define it.

Anti-Gunners use the term "assault weapon" because it has become synonymous with mass killings. THANKS MEDIA. The truth is, more mass killings are committed with handguns than rifles. So if your anti-gun friend's "assault weapon" rant goes any further than this you can give them this statistic.

FBI Statistics show knives are used to kill people 7 times more than rifles. So, how do you justify your so-called "assault weapon" ban but propose nothing related to knives?

But the Anti-Gunners love their "assault weapon" drama.

Another small victory you can give them is to agree with them when they claim to want to "save lives." The truth is, they don't want to save lives as much as they want to ban guns, but play along.

"We just want to save lives and prevent innocent people from getting killed." Your response:

I totally agree. That is a noble cause. (That's their win.) **So why then do you try to disarm people and make them helpless in an attack? That's what gun restrictions do. You don't want to be responsible for people not being able to defend themselves, do you?**

I understand you want to save lives. So do I, but did you know that 4 times as many people die from drunk-driving related accidents than do from firearm related homicides? What efforts have you made to prevent drunk-driving? This response is to expose the Anti-Gunners hypocrisy. Remember, they don't really care about saving lives as much as the want to ban guns.

"We need to get these assault weapons off the streets and end this senseless bloodshed!"

I agree we need to end senseless bloodshed but it's not because of guns. I can't understand how making good people unarmed and helpless will help them survive an attack. You see, gun-restrictions make good people vulnerable while making the killer's job easier. So can you explain to me how this is supposed to work?

1. Don't give a damn about their feelings
2. Expose their lack of common sense
3. Insult their intelligence
4. Keep them on the receiving end of the question

5. Attack first
6. Expose their immorality
7. Frame them as the bad guy or the enemy
8. Stay focused and stay out of their traps
9. Keep them on your agenda
10. Give them small victories but expose their illogic.
11. Relax

The anti-gun crowd loves to distort the position of gun-owners. It's most often the only way they can win the argument. Often times, the gun-conversation turns into a war of words and statistics. But when the anti-gunners put their Bloomberg funded "statistics" that have been reported in Huffington Post and "fact-checked" by Snopes up against FBI data, their argument takes a nose dive. So, what is a good anti-gunner to do when they know they need to recruit people, but they don't have the facts on their side?

They use what is called a "Strawman" argument. An anti-gun Strawman argument is a total distortion of what gun-owners actually think. It's important to the anti-gun crowd to misrepresent the pro-gun position in a way that is easy to ridicule, mock and make look foolish. By distorting gun owners' argument or position, it makes it easier to discredit. Here's are some examples of distorted gun-owner's positions or "Strawman" arguments.

The first one is a common argument, misrepresenting the pro-gun position for the sake of making gun-owners appear reckless. The second one is an actual posting found on

Facebook for the purpose of making gun-owners appear irrational and fearful.

1. *"You gun-owners want every teacher to be armed to the teeth. I'm sorry, but making teachers carry guns against their will in the classroom is dangerous."*

     The reason this distorted representation is so dangerous, is that is implies that gun-owners want to pass out guns and force people, who wouldn't know how to use them, to carry them around all day. This couldn't be further from the truth and the anti-gun crowd knows this, but the perception of those listening to the argument is the target. In other words, it doesn't matter if the argument is honest, as long as it paints an ugly picture of gun-owners in the minds of those who are watching but not paying close attention.

2. *"I'm seeing so much on Facebook about Red Flag Laws. As it turns out, 100% of everything I've read on Facebook about Red Flag Laws is untrue. No, they cannot sneak into your house without your knowledge, search in the middle of the night while you sleep in your bed. This is false. The police will always make their presence known, and if there are people in the house, those people will be moved to one location or asked to leave the residence if not detained. They will not search your house while you are laying in bed. No, you are not subject to seizure of your guns for being a Trump supporter. This is false."*

This is a very clever "Strawman" because it implies that gun owners actually believe police will be sneaking around in their houses in the middle of the night while they sleep. Ask any gun-owner if they think like this and you will get a resounding no. This type of thought process is more likely a notion conjured up in the minds of anti-gunners. This statement paints a vivid picture of gun-owners being fearful, irrational and suspicious. Not a good look and the anti-gun crowd knows it. That's why they do it.

When people are confronted with a Strawman argument, the natural inclination is to defend against it. The problem with defending against a false representation of your position is that it implies ownership of the position. That's what the anti-gun crowd is trying to achieve. Because of our natural reaction to defend ourselves, the anti-gun crowd is able to position gun-owners the way they want, ultimately creating a false public perception. Unfortunately, gun-owners often fall into the trap when they defend the fake position the anti-gunner created.

By understanding this strategy, we are much less likely to argue a position that the anti-gunners fabricate. The best way to respond to the dishonest "Strawman" strategy is to avoid defending it while shining a spotlight on it for all to see.

A good response to a Strawman argument may be:

"You either need to distort my position because you can't win the argument with the lies you've been fed, or you don't really understand my position at all. Which one is it?"

11. THE COST OF GUN-CONTROL

It's not so unbelievable that a government would want to disarm its citizens, but that American citizens would beg to be disarmed by their government is a much scarier thought.

The Gun-Free Zone is a microcosm of the "Socialist-Utopia," Democrats dream of.

A recent Crime Prevention Research Center study showed, violent killers seek out Gun-Free Zones 94% of the time. So, why would Politicians refuse to re-evaluate their support of these deadly areas, even after seeing the massacres that they cause? First, we need to look at their decades-long commitment to gun-control. From the lowest ranks of the Beto O'Rourkes, all the way up to Presidents, we have seen a relentless push for gun control, regardless of the deadly effects gun-restrictions show us time and time again.

Two common elements that fuel the ignorant push for Gun-Free Zones are the perceived intellectual superiority of the Gun-Grabbers and a denial or ignorance of the American spirit. The intellectuals who continue to believe that a government-controlled Utopia can be created in America could never admit that their ideas are flawed. They truly believe that in the end they will create the government controlled Socialist-Utopia they've always dreamed of. Many of these people have been taught from birth that they are intellectually superior. So how could they ever admit that their ideas are dangerous and delusional, and if they did, what would that say about them?

The Anti-2nd Amendment Radicals in Congress, left-wing media and anti-gun lobbying groups like Moms Demand Action and Everytown for Gun Safety watch people die in these deadly zones while ignoring their own culpability. They stand on graves while pushing their agenda and use the death-toll numbers to gain more support for gun-control. Their belief that they know what is best gives them false-license to ignore reality and continue to put people in danger by making them unarmed and helpless. They have studied the strategies and tactics other Governments have used on people to enforce compliance and they believe they will be able to do the same. But they fail to see one very important element, one that if not singularly unique to America, it is extremely strong in the hearts and cultural DNA of most Americans due to the nature of our founding.

The Gun-Grabbers don't understand the strength of the American spirit because it is something that they have lost (or never had to begin with.) The passion for freedom, liberty and individualism, runs through the veins of the majority of Americans, but it is completely lost on some. Patriotism and the willingness of real Americans to fight against tyranny (again, if we must) is the biggest roadblock faced by the Socialists living among us. Our founding fathers wrote the Constitution and Bill of Rights with their own blood, but some of the people we put in charge to defend those documents, have been taught to believe they are irrelevant.

If those who support the Utopian experimental laboratories known as Gun-Free Zones were to admit that they are a dreadful failure, they would also have to admit that their idea of a government-controlled Utopian America is a fantasy. So, rather than acknowledge the blood on their hands, they push for more Gun-Free Zones and watch people get slaughtered while continuing to tell themselves that they are much smarter than everyone else.

Why do we expect people, who can't conceptualize freedom, to defend freedom?

What is control and why do some people seek it, while others resist it? It's hard to believe that we even utter the word "socialism" in America, but the brutal truth is that some people desperately need to control society and socialism has become an acceptable concept, in their minds, to achieve that.

Let's first look at the definition of control, in its verb and noun context.

Control – verb
con·trol | \ kən-'trōl
controlled; controlling
: to exercise restraining or directing influence over
: to regulate
: to have power over

Control - noun
: an act or instance of controlling
: power or authority to guide or manage

What causes some people to seek control? We've all sought control over things in life. It's necessary when managing things like our finances, organizing our households, traffic and many other instances that make our lives better, safer and more predictable but what happens in

203

the minds of those who want to control *other people*? When we talk about freedom, we usually mean the ability to live our lives absent of any restrictions or control implemented by others. It's clear that some in government like the idea of controlling society and they are very good at selling the concept to those who like the idea of *being* controlled. Like we talked about in Chapter 8 (Safe Space) there is a market for control and Democrats have it locked up. What I want to get to, is the thought-process of those who seek it. We already can assume that those who want to *be* controlled, want it for a sense of safety and the elimination of responsibility but where do the *controllers* get their desire to control people and how is it that the need to control others grows beyond their own personal space?

When my son was young, my wife and I would watch him like a hawk, primarily because he got into everything and we didn't want him getting hurt, but I started to notice an anxiety when I didn't know where he was or I couldn't see him. Many parents will understand this especially if they have a child who can crawl faster than a greased bullet. It was that anxiety that I am most interested in because it caused us to be extra vigilant. I know many people will say, *"there's nothing wrong with keeping an eye on a young child"* and that's true but what caused the anxiety? The answer is easy. Fear. In our case, it was fear of the unknown. In other words, when we didn't know where our son was, we were afraid he was getting into something dangerous. It's why the "child monitor" was invented.

What happens to a parent's level of anxiety or fear when they are able to look at a screen or listen to a monitor and see or hear their child safely playing in the other room? The fear goes away because the "unknown" is now "known." There is a sense of control in "knowing" because you have the data which gives you leverage over the situation. In other words, you can now physically manipulate the situation because you have the information. The ability to physically change the situation relieves the fear of something bad happening.

How does this relate to politics? I believe there are some with political power that fear society going in a direction they don't like so they seek the ability to control it with laws, rules, restrictions and constant oversight. This may come from an inherent need to quell their fear and anxiety or it may come from a lack of trust that people will do the right thing if given the option. That speaks to their own fear and doubt in themselves, because in order to believe others would make a poor choice under certain circumstances, you likely believe you would make the same choices given the same circumstance. We always imagine we know what others would do, but it is really what we fear we would do in a given situation. The thoughts we project onto other, come from our own mind.

People want to know what is going on and they believe that with more laws, others will fall in line and obey the standards that have been set for them. This, they may think will help in organizing society and should people fall out of line, laws are in place to punish the offenders and condition them to never do it again. Kind of like a child who continues to draw on the wall or a dog who chews the couch. Some think that others watching will see people being punished and refrain from committing the same violation. This is control but unlike the baby-monitor, this type of control is used on a large scale and punishment by force is the deterrent. There are also some who want control for financial reasons. Ugly, I know, but an inherent human trait

When our Founding Fathers set the stage for the evolution of America, they were smart enough to recognize this important human feature, or defect, depending on how you look at it. This is why the Bill of Rights was written. They knew that people would seek to control other people so they put that power in the hands of "We the People" and made it clear that the government was never to have the ability to wield control over the people who employed them. Unfortunately, the inherent need to "control" has become overwhelmingly intense in the minds of some, to the point that they fight to take freedom away from people on a daily basis. There are some living among us that are more than happy to give their freedom to a government that may not have the best interest of the people in mind.

In America, the radical left uses imagery and talking points to compare republicans and conservatives to Nazis, but when you look at the strategies of Hitler and his regime, you find more correlation between Nazis and the radical American Left.

After the German army's retreat in World War I, Hitler blamed the defeat on right-wing propaganda and vowed to restore Germany's reputation. He would eventually have power and use the power of propaganda himself. After 4 years of war, Hitler returned to Germany and wanted to stay in the Army because he liked the idea of order & stability and he wanted to support the new social-Democrat President Friedrich Ebert.

Upon Hitler's rise to political power he made his announcement to name his party the National Socialist German Worker's Party (Nazi). Hitler made it known that he was in favor of Socialism. He was also able to galvanize a small group of radicals and started making it a point to express his anti-semitic and anti-capitalism views. The picture of someone who wanted control was starting to become very clear and his support grew ten-fold in one year. This shows just how easily some people will gravitate toward those who take control of society if they believe the messaging.

The Nazi party soon developed it's own propaganda newspaper called The Racist People's Observer. It was backed financially by Hitler's supporters and effectively controlled the narrative. Alfred Rosenberg was an anti-Semite and also the paper's editor. He played a huge role in Hitler's ability to dominate the people because he had great influence in shaping the thought-process of his readers and inspired the shape of the new Nazi ideology. They would only get the information Hitler and his regime wanted them to get and this would guide the people to believe that what *they* stood for was honorable. They would also believe that anyone who opposed them was the enemy. Does this sound at all familiar to some American "news" outlets?

In a desperate attempt to gain control, and under extreme financial pressure put on Germany by the French, Hitler was able to acquire guns and other weaponry. He would then convince his followers to oppose the German Police. The Nazis were far outnumbered and ultimately failed but the anger Hitler was able to instill in his people was enough to get them to put their own lives on the line in support of the Nazi ideology and overall mission. Many Nazis died at the hands of police and Hitler would hold ceremonies in their honor. The people would be forced to participate in these ceremonies for years later. Hitler would finally get the power he wanted. He was able to gain control by acquiring support in numbers through consistent propaganda, rituals, enforced celebrations and other forms of leverage. He acquired ideological loyalty.

Hitler would soon be arrested and accused of high treason but sympathetic judges and overwhelming public support resulted in him getting a very easy sentence. During his almost hotel-like jail accommodations Hitler started to read Carl Marx and he wrote his own biography that would soon be considered the bible of National Socialism (Nazism) in Germany's Third Reich. Hitler would then take power in 1933, not long after the financial crash of 1929. He knew that during times of economic success, his chances to gain support were much less likely. Socialist views thrive when people have less confidence in their financial future, which would seem to be very well played by left-wing American politicians.

Without financial strife, the politicians don't have the opportunity to offer government solutions in exchange for control over the lives of the people. This is why some politicians refuse to acknowledge a booming economy and continue to push "Doom and Gloom." People aren't encouraged to look for government support when they know they can make it on their own. Democrats in America rely on poverty and the fear of poverty for voter support.

Hitler's socialist views were soon embraced by his followers, thanks partly to a failed economy and the propaganda he perpetuated. Hitler's ideological views were pushed on the people through newspapers and most importantly his own writings. Should someone choose not to read his book "Mein Kampf" or comply with his doctrine, they would be shunned and often punished. This was the beginning of the indoctrination on a mass level. During that time over 18,000,000 copies of Hitler's book were sold and copies were given to newly married couples and soldiers. Not only did this make Hitler very rich but it solidified his views in the minds of the people. Some would argue that this type of indoctrination into the Nazi ideology is similar to the way American liberal-progressives are encouraged to adopt the ideology of the Left. The strategies are similar in many ways with respect to the powerful media and educational components along with the ability of internet companies to control content. "Intolerance" would also appear to be a necessary component when controlling people. How strong would a political message be if it's leaders waivered or compromised?

Hitler's army of mostly young men grew to 170,000 over a short period of time and soon after that reached numbers over 400,000. Large donations were made by wealthy business owners such as Henry Ford. Hitler's personal photographer was complicit in taking strategically staged photographs to depict the Nazis in a desirable light while creating a less desirable view of anyone who opposed. The Soros backed Antifa and other radical left-wing groups in America with help from some main-stream media outlets seem to resemble this same type of media-manipulation. Nazi and ANTFA similarities are apparent right down to the armbands and their opposition to the police. Probably just a coincidence, so let's not jump to any conclusions just yet.

At the time of Hitler's inevitable rise to power, President Hindenburg refused to name Hitler, Chancellor. Hindenburg said, *"Before God, my conscience and the Fatherland, I cannot hand over power to a party as intolerant as yours."* In 1933, Hitler was ultimately named Chancellor and he branded his new cabinet with the name "The Cabinet of National Concentration."

Hitler knew the power of emotion. He knew that if he could slant the narrative, brainwash the people and use their fear and hatred against them, he would be able to garner their support. In a speech he said, *"The masses are feminine and stupid. Only emotion and hatred can keep them under control."* This would seem to position his supporters as the minority and encourage them that facts have no place where reactive-emotion is present. Similar to the anti-gun left in America, Hitler used fear and hatred to motivate his support and gain control. Nazi thugs openly bullied people in the streets because they were taught that they were justified in their actions. Sound familiar? There have been countless numbers of radical leftists doing the same in recent years. The difference now, is the ability to capture their actions on video.

So why did Hitler need to control the people so badly? Why did the people under him so easily oblige? Hitler's reign of power and his supporter's willingness to be dominated by a ruthless dictator was a match made in Hell. Both got something out of the deal. Adolf Hitler was able to satisfy his own need to control society and his people were able to live under leadership that would take care of all their needs, or so they initially thought.

During 2019, as a whole slew of Democratic hopefuls lined up to take a shot at the Presidency, the messaging all seemed to resemble that of a government control/citizen dominated ideology. When the topic of guns came up, regardless of which candidate was at the microphone, the message was always that of gun-control or some sort of confiscation. Eric Swalwell seemed to tout the most dictatorial ideals of the bunch. I'm not saying Swalwell is Hitler but his views seem completely devoid of anything resembling freedom. I am not suggesting that Swalwell is the only one who takes a top-down approach. Beto O'Rourke called for the out-right confiscation of guns, should he become President. This is a very common component within the Left's ideological views.

When Anti-2nd Amendment Radicals push gun-control laws, they want you to think their intention is to save lives, but when we look at how these laws would violate the rights of people and put them in danger, we begin to understand their real motives. When anyone wants others to be vulnerable, we have to ask ourselves, how it is that the perpetrator might benefit. In this case, the perpetrator being those who try to gain leverage over the citizens.

During his attempts at winning the Democratic primaries, Congressman Eric Swalwell held a rally in 2019 that attracted approximately 20 people. At this rally, he unveiled his list of gun-control measures that he would implement should he become President. The good news is, he was one of the first to drop out of the race. His performance took place outside the NRA Headquarters in Virginia (for effect). His list of attacks on the citizens he hoped to represent as President included civil liberties violations that cause the gun-grabbers to salivate, but when we look at the potential results of his ideas, we get a good idea of what his real intentions might be. Here are some of the things Swalwell proposed.

- **Ban and "buy back" so-called "semi-automatic assault weapons" and prosecute those who don't comply**

  This is confiscation under the guise of "buy-back." As soon as "prosecution for not complying" enters the equation, the freedom to choose is eliminated and our "rights" are gone. This is the thinking of a dictator.

- **Implement background checks for all gun and ammunition purchases**

  Studies have shown that 90% of criminals surveyed in prison, acquired their firearms illegally and avoided background checks, while 95% of background checks denied are initially "false positives" (good people being unjustly denied). If the gun-grabbers know that criminals pay no attention to background checks but good people are the ones denied, who are these background checks really intended for?

- **Create a federal licensing program for gun owners, requiring them to satisfactorily complete a training program with both written and practical exams, the same way most states do with cars and hunters.**

  This would appear to be another way to limit gun-ownership by giving bureaucrats the ability to create required standards that would be impossible to meet. Who do you think would write the rules to these mandatory programs or the questions on these mandatory exams?

- **Require that all people or businesses selling more than 1,000 rounds of ammunition in a 30-day period be federally licensed in a program similar to the Federal Firearms Licensee system.**

  This could be an attempt at implementing another government issued license created and run by those who don't want firearms dealers in the first place.

Firearms dealers would have to meet additional government standards, ultimately making it more difficult for them to conduct business, running most of them out of business and sending the firearms industry underground.

- **Prohibit individuals from "hoarding" ammunition in quantities exceeding 200 rounds per caliber or gauge.**

200 rounds is hardly "hoarding" but any terminology that makes gun-owners look dangerous is helpful to the anti-gun agenda. This would appear to be rhetoric on the surface but if implemented, would limit the ability of gun-owners to train; turning gun-ranges into ghost towns and creating an ammo drought that would prevent people the ability to defend themselves if attacked. Guns would collect dust in closets because there would be no sense in carrying one if it was ammo-less. A law like this would conveniently criminalize anyone who owns more than 200 rounds. But how would they ever know how much ammo you have? That's what the ammo background checks are for. Under these policies, ammo would be tracked.

- **Limit ammunition sales for individual purchasers to 200 rounds per 30-day period.**

Again, the lack of ammo would shut down gun ranges causing a lack of interest in future generations. If no one can shoot for practice or recreation, the desire for these activities will quickly disappear. This, coupled with a continued effort to implement gun-fear in our youth would make gun-ownership a thing of the past as our youth became less familiar with guns over the coming generations.

- **Repeal the law that prohibits the U.S. Bureau of Alcohol, Tobacco, Firearms and Explosives from consolidating and centralizing records relating to the acquisition of firearms maintained by federal firearms licensees.**

In other words: "Gun-Owner Database." I'm not sure if there is any other way to see this one. Remember the Red Flag Laws that many states are trying to implement and ask yourself how they would work hand-in-hand with a database.

- **48 Hour "cooling off" period for firearm purchases.**

The biggest problem with this is the fact that people would be vulnerable to attacks during waiting periods. Women being stalked or pursued by a violent predator would have to "wait it out."

The idea that someone would need time to "cool off" or they would otherwise kill is an idea that lives in the minds of Anti-Gunners and Anti-2nd Amendment Radicals. By believing *others* would act dangerously when angered or "triggered," they may be revealing more about *themselves* than they realize. This is a common projection that comes from the irrational gun-fear crowd that believes *"guns make people do bad things."* This reveals their own dangerously volatile lack of physical restraint. Someone who thinks *other people* need 48 hours to "decide not to kill someone," may have some deeper issues that need to be addressed. Either you can control your own actions, or you can't. Maybe these gun-grabbers should propose a 48 hour "cooling off" period to Antifa members when they attempt to purchase, chains, padlocks, crowbars, 2 by 4's, pepper spray and face masks. Instead, the same people who want a "cooling off" period for lawful gun-owners, support the efforts of radical leftist groups.

- **Prohibit states from allowing teachers to be armed on campus.**

Preventing teachers from being able to protect themselves and their kids would only seem to perpetuate the dangerous activity we continue to see in Gun Free School Zones. If the idea is to *prevent* senseless killings in schools, how does it make sense to purposely make teachers and students more vulnerable? It would seem that this type of policy would encourage *more* school attacks, ultimately justifying the call for more gun-laws, but I'm sure that's not the intent here. Nobody is that sick.

- **Require that liability insurance be purchased before a person can buy, trade, or otherwise receive**

a firearm, which is what states already require for automobiles.

This looks like yet another way to eliminate gun-ownership in America by pitting insurance companies against gun-owners. How soon would there only be one insurance company left willing to provide this insurance and how expensive would it be? Would a law like this encourage frivolous lawsuits against gun-owners? How would it help to offer monetary rewards to people for suing gun-owners? What would happen if your insurance policy lapsed? Would the insurance company be required to notify the government, similar to the way insurance companies now notify DMV if your car insurance lapses? If Government was notified upon your insurance lapsing, what would they do about it? Comparing this policy to automobile insurance a way of justifying it. This is a way to make is seem like a "common sense policy" so you look irrational if you don't go along with it.

The ironic thing about each and every one of Swalwell's proposals is that the people we need to be concerned with would never follow a single one of them. Only the law-abiding gun-owners would be affected. So who would these policies be intended for?

If only the Anti-Gunners could see how voting for this type of government overreach would likely affect them on issues *they* care about down the road. If we find ourselves telling them, "*See, we told you so,*" it'll already be too late.

In another example of what would seem to be blatant "gun-grabbing" intent, at a Town Hall meeting in Deerfield Illinois, Anti-Gun Senator Julie Morrison looked a bit frustrated when Town Hall Attendee, Mike Weisman pointed out the hypocrisy in her gun policy.

Senator Julie Morrison (D-29) sponsored Senate Bill 107 which would essentially criminalize the ownership of many commonly owned semi-automatic rifles, shotguns and handguns by qualifying them as "assault weapons."

Some examples of the Senator's "banned" firearms would include:

- **Any semi-automatic rifle or handgun that can accept a detachable magazine greater than ten rounds in capacity and has one or more features, such as a protruding grip for the support hand; a folding, telescoping, or thumbhole stock; a handguard; or a muzzle brake or compensator.**

(Cute wording in this one: "Any semi-automatic rifle or handgun that can **accept** *a detachable magazine greater than ten rounds in capacity." ...They all can.)*

- **Any semi-automatic shotgun that has one or more feature such as the ability to accept a detachable magazine; a folding, telescoping, or thumbhole stock; or a protruding grip for the support hand.**

- **Any fixed magazine semi-automatic rifles or handguns greater than ten rounds in capacity and fixed magazine semi-automatic shotguns greater than five rounds in capacity.**

- Any shotgun with a revolving cylinder.

- Any part or accessory that would configure a firearm as above

SB 107 would have limited exemptions, such as allowing those who already lawfully own the newly banned firearms to keep them as long as they register them and pay a fee. This exemption would seem to imply that upon paying a fee and letting government officials know who owns these guns and where they are located, ownership would be ok.

Town Hall attendee, Mike Weisman was smarter than Senator Morrison would have preferred because he pointed out this hypocrisy when he asked the gun-grabbing Senator,

"If I get to keep it, if I pay a fine and register it, then how dangerous is it in the first place and why do you need to ban it at all?"

This implied that Senator Morrison is not really concerned with the safety of her constituents. It has been proven time and time again that the banning of any type of firearm does not reduce crime and you would think Senator Morrison knows it. This question just exposed what would appear to be the Senator's desire to control gun-owners and capitalize monetarily off of gun-ownership. Senator Morrison didn't seem to like Mike Weisman's question because it poked a giant hole right through the center of her dishonest gun-grab attempt and she had quite the revealing response. While casually leaning on a podium with her head tilted back just enough so she could look down her nose at Mr. Weisman, she pushed her tongue into her cheek and with a sarcastic, demeaning tone similar to the way a parent would calmly and authoritatively scold a child, she said:

"Well, you've just maybe changed my mind. Maybe we won't have a fine at all. Maybe there'll just be a confiscation and we won't have to worry about having a fine."

Then the over-confident Senator looked to her supporters and smugly smiled. Illinois Representative Bob Morgan quickly tried to clean up the messy and very revealing statement made by the irresponsible Senator but the damage had been done, or should I say, the true colors had been revealed.

When the Anti-2ⁿᵈ Amendment Radicals say, *"Nobody wants to take your guns,"* they are lying. The arrogance that comes with the belief that they *can* take guns from Americans is the scary part. When they say, *"Nobody wants to take your guns,"* the implication is that they have the power to do so, and the hope is that you trust them not to.

AFTERWORD

Thanks so much for reading. I hope I was able to offer you some value and I hope this conversation continues in grocery stores, waiting rooms, coffee shops and at dinner tables across America. I'll bet, if we each take one action everyday with the intent of showing someone else the importance of Amendment #2, we will find ourselves in America again.

So what are you going to do now? Will you take action to preserve the 2nd Amendment or will you put this book down and hope someone else takes care of it?

I know, I know, you think you can't possibly make a difference amidst the constant attacks from the anti-gun crowd. I know what you're thinking, *"They keep implementing more rules and regulations, they're constantly walking on the Constitution and making it more difficult to be a gun owner. It pisses me off!"*

So… what then?

The 2nd Amendment is not a privilege. It's your right.

Dan Wos

http://www.goodgunbadguy.net

http://www.danwos.com
http://www.goodgunbadguy.blogspot.com

SUMMARY OF STATISTICS
From Good Gun Bad Guy 1, 2 and 3

- FBI-Number of gun related deaths in America (2012): 8,855
- IIHS-Number of auto related deaths in America (2012): 33,561
- CDC-Average number of cigarette related deaths per year in America: 480,000

Other causes of deaths:
- Overexertion - 10 per year
- Getting cut or punctured - 105 per year
- Bicycling – 242 per year
- Machinery – 590 per year
- Accidental Firearms – 606 per year
- Getting struck – 788 per year
- Other forms of transportation – 857 per year
- Pedestrian activity – 1074 per year
- Natural / Environmental – 1576 per year
- Fires / Burning 2845 per year
- Drowning – 3782 per year
- Unspecified – 5688 per year
- Suffocation – 6165 per year
- Falling – 26009 per year
- Poisoning – 33041 per year
- Automobile – 33561 per year

Gun-Control leads to People-Control

- 1911, Turkey enacted gun control and soon after killed 1.5 million Armenians
- 1929, The Soviet Union enacted gun control and over the next 24 years killed approximately 20 million who opposed government policy.
- 1935, China enacted gun control and killed 20 million political dissidents within 17 years.
- 1938, Germany enacted gun control and killed 13 million Jews in the 7 years that followed.
- 1956, Cambodia enacted gun control and killed 1 million people by 1977
- 1964, Guatemala enacted gun control and killed 100,000 Mayan Indians by 1981
- 1970, Uganda enacted gun control and by 1979 300,000 Christians were killed.

1,165,383 people (in the year 2014 alone) were the victims of violent crimes -FBI 2014 Crime Statistics, released September 28, 2015

- *Gun Free Zones have been the target of more than 94% of all mass shootings – Crime Prevention Research Center. (Anti-Gun Groups support GFZ's)*

- *Guns are used 2.46 million time per year in America to save lives – Centers for Disease Control (report was hidden from the public for 20 years)*

- *90% of criminals surveyed in jail, admitted to avoiding background checks when acquiring firearms – Department of Justice study.*

The **Gun-Free School Zones Act** (GFSZA) is a federal United States law that prohibits any unauthorized individual from knowingly possessing a firearm at a place that the individual knows, or has reasonable cause to believe, is a school zone as defined by 18 U.S.C. § 921(a)(25). Such a firearm has to move in or affect interstate or foreign commerce for the ban to be effective. It was introduced in the U.S. Senate in October 1990 by Joseph R. Biden and signed into law in November 1990 by George H. W. Bush. The Gun-Free School Zones Act of 1990 was originally passed as section 1702 of the Crime Control Act of 1990.

A Stanford University study found that killers choose Gun-Free-Zones 69% of the time. 29% of the attacks where citizens where allowed to carry a firearm were stopped or slowed down by a Good Guy with a gun.

Firearms are used for self-defense between 2.1 and 2.5 million times per year. In over 1.9 million of these cases, a handgun was used – From "Armed Resistance to Crime": The Prevalence and Nature of Self-Defense with a Gun. Published in the Northwestern University School of Law's Journal of Criminal Law and Criminology, 1995

In the State of Florida 1.3 million people are legally licensed to carry a gun. That is approximately 6.5% of the State's population.

In November 2015 the U.S. Court of Appeals for the D.C. Circuit issued a win against over-reaching government. The decision struck down four provisions of D.C. firearms law and handed justice to law abiding gun owners of Washington D.C.

In the *Heller v. District of Columbia* lawsuit, the 4 key provisions that were struck down are:

- The court overturned the limitation on registration of one handgun per month.

- The court struck down the three-year re-registration requirement, which imposed a never-ending burden on gun owners in the District.

- The court invalidated the requirement that the registrant physically bring the firearm to police headquarters to register it.

- The court struck down the requirement that applicants pass a test on D.C. gun laws, citing the lack of any public safety benefit.

The National Crime Victimization Survey conducted by the Department of Justice released some interesting data. Women have a 2.5 times greater chance of sustaining serious injury when offering no resistance to a violent criminal as opposed to using a firearm for self-defense. However, men have only a 1.4 times greater chance of sustaining injuries for playing a passive role. That means taking an active role and protecting oneself pays off on average twice as much for women.

From 1999-2007 the number of permit holders grew at an average rate of 237,500 per year. During the Obama administration the number of new permit holders averaged 850,000 per year.

The FBI reported that on Black Friday in 2015 it had processed the most background checks for gun purchases ever recorded in one single day; this, just after the November 13th Paris attacks and more gun restriction rhetoric and threats from President Obama. The number of background checks peaked at an unprecedented 185,345. The total number of background checks for the month of November, 2015 hit 2,243,030; one of the highest months on record.

Year	FBI reported firearm deaths	NICS background checks
2009	9,199	14,033,824
2010	8,874	14,409,616
2011	8,653	16,454,951
2012	8,897	19,592,303
2013	8,454	21,093,273
2014	8,124	20,968,547

One year after the Australian ban, it was determined by a Harvard study that, Australian "suicides by gun" went down by 57%. But the suicide *rate* reached a ten-year high. This tells us that although people had less access to guns, it did nothing to deter suicides. As a matter of fact, they increased. Anti-Gunners only recite the 57% reduction in "suicides by gun" because that part fits their narrative.

While Australia's rate of violent crime has peaked in the years following its ban, the United States experienced the exact opposite phenomenon. One year after gun owners in Australia were forced by law to surrender their 640,381 personal firearms, (which were destroyed) new statistics were calculated. The mandatory gun buy-back program cost Australian taxpayers over $500 million dollars and resulted in a 3.2% increase in homicides, 8.6% increase in assaults and a 44% increase in armed robberies.

In addition to required drop testing, there are a number of safety features installed in firearms to further prevent misfires. Some of them include:

- Thumb safety
- Trigger safety
- Grip safety
- Hammer safety
- Glock Safe Action System
- Firing pin block
- Hammer block
- Transfer bar
- Safety notch

- Magazine disconnect
- De-cocker

An additional "safety feature" that gets a bit of controversy is the "long hard trigger press" such as the NY1 8lb trigger and the NY2 12lb trigger. Some law enforcement officers are required to use these heavy triggered guns. The common complaint is that accuracy is greatly diminished and some even argue that this attempt at making guns safer is not an improvement but a dangerous feature because it compromises the accuracy of the shooter.

Some estimates say there are over 350,000,000 guns in our population of approximately 319,000,000 people.

The Crime Prevention Research Center (CPRC) reported an 18% decrease in crime during the time period between 2007-2015. This is particularly interesting because during that same time period handgun carry permits rose 190%.

190% increase in handgun permits = 18% decrease in crime.

(2016) brought the largest (1) year increase in new carry permits. The 2016 all-time record was an increase of 1.8 million new handgun permits. The closest, prior to that, was the year before in 2015, which brought 1.73 million new permit holders. It is no coincidence that during these (2) years of massive increases in handgun permits, the country was counteracting countless assaults to our 2nd Amendment by the Obama Administration and state governments across the country.

Some will say former President Obama was America's best gun-salesman.

Outside of California and New York, you can count on at least 8% of any State's population to be licensed to carry. (11) States have at least 10% of their population licensed to own and carry firearms. Indiana boasts 15.8% carriers and our friends in Alabama have approximately 20% of their residents licensed to carry.

1 out of 10 people could potentially be a Good Guy or Gal with a gun.

In 2016 the FBI firearms background checks (which roughly represents gun sales) reached 27,538,673. This number is approximately 4,000,000 more than were recorded in 2015 and is almost double the number of background checks recorded in President Obama's first year in office. Since Donald Trump's election, a sigh of relief was heard around the country and as a result, gun-sales slipped just a bit. Sales for December 2016 did not meet the same 3.3 million background checks they did in December of 2015. This activity speaks directly to the confidence Americans have with President Trump's stance on 2nd Amendment issues.

- Gallup survey says 43 percent of people in America have a gun in the house.

- NRA-ILA says 40-45 percent of households have firearms.

Constitutional-Carry States as of 2019

- **Alaska** – Became a Constitutional-Carry state in 2003
- **Arizona** – Became a Constitutional-Carry state in 2010
- **Arkansas** – Became a Constitutional-Carry state in 2013
- **Idaho** – Became a Constitutional-Carry state in 2016
- **Kansas** – Became a Constitutional-Carry state in 2015
- **Kentucky** – Became a Constitutional -Carry state in 2019
- **Maine** – Became a Constitutional-Carry state in 2015
- **Mississippi** – Became a Constitutional-Carry state in 2016
- **Missouri** – Became a Constitutional-Carry state in 2016
- **Montana** – Became a Constitutional-Carry State in 2011
- **New Hampshire** – Became a Constitutional-Carry state in 2017
- **North Dakota** – Became a Constitutional-Carry state in 2017
- **Oklahoma** – Became a Constitutional-Carry state in 2019
- **South Dakota** – Became a Constitutional-Carry state in 2019
- **Vermont** – Has never required a permit or license
- **West Virginia** – Became a Constitutional-Carry state in 2016
- **Wyoming** – Became a Constitutional-Carry state in 2011

*Montana State law exempts a concealed carrier from the prohibition on concealed carry if he or she is "outside the official boundaries of a city or town or the confines of a logging, lumbering, mining, or railroad camp or who is lawfully engaged in hunting, fishing, trapping, camping, hiking, backpacking, farming, ranching, or other outdoor activity in which weapons are often carried for recreation or protection."

According to the chief gun lobbyist in the state of Montana, Gary Marbut, 99.4% of the state is outside city limits (and he gets that information from the Montana League of Cities and Towns). So virtually the entire state enjoys permit-less carry. And Marbut's organization, the Montana Shooting Sports Alliance, considers Montana a Constitutional Carry state.

Of the 5,100 violent gun-related deaths per year, 1,276 (approximately 25%) come from four very gun-restrictive cities.

- **Chicago, IL 480 homicides (9.4%)**
- **Baltimore, MD 344 homicides (6.7%)**
- **Detroit, MI 333 homicides (6.5%)**
- **Washington, D.C. 119 homicides (2.3%)**

- **30,000 gun-related deaths**
- **19,500 suicide**
- **5,100 homicide**
- **4,500 law-enforcement related**
- **900 accidental discharge**

Of those 5,100 homicides:

- **480 Chicago**
- **344 Baltimore**
- **333 Detroit**
- **119 Washington, D.C.**

Accidental child-deaths (pool vs. gun, under 15 yrs. Old)

- **83 yearly child-related pool deaths per 8,079,000 households with pools.**
- **86 yearly child-related gun deaths per 45,000,000 households with guns.**
- **1 gun to every 6 pool deaths (children)**

  Note: the number of households with guns was likely much higher than surveyed, which would result in the number of swimming pools deaths being much higher in comparison.

According to FBI statistics, violent crime was up 8.6% in the U.S. in 2016, from 2015. 20% of the 2016 8.6% increase in violent crime nationwide can be attributed to Chicago alone.

2019 States with Red Flag Laws include:

- Connecticut
- Indiana
- California
- Washington
- Oregon
- Colorado
- Florida
- Vermont
- Maryland
- Rhode Island
- New Jersey
- Delaware
- Massachusetts
- Illinois
- New York
- Nevada
- Hawaii

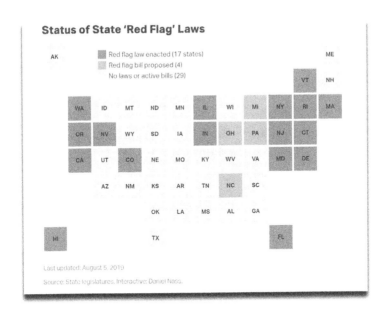

Status of State 'Red Flag' Laws

Red flag law enacted (17 states)
Red flag bill proposed (4)
No laws or active bills (29)

Last updated: August 5, 2019

Source: State legislatures. Interactive: Daniel Nass.

Police Response Times:

City	Population	Police response Time (minutes)
San Francisco, CA.	884,363	5.46
Houston, TX	2,312,717	5.51
Los Angeles, CA	3,999,759	6.1
New York City, NY	8,622,698	6.69
San Antonio, TX	1,511,946	6.88
Austin, TX	950,715	7.15
Dallas, TX	1,341,075	8.39
Seattle, WA	724,745	9
San Jose, CA	1,035,317	9.2
Fort Worth, TX	874,168	9.5

90% of criminals surveyed by the DOJ said they avoid background checks for gun purchases. 95% of background check denials are initially false positives. 67,500 good people are denied their 2nd Amendment right every year.

FBI statistics show rifles to be used in gun-related killings less than 5% of the time, compared to handguns. Knives are used to kill people 7 times more than rifles.

FBI statistics show rifles make up only 2% if all gun related crime.

There are just over 300 million people in America (326,000,000 in 2017). There are just over 1 million successful violent crimes in America per year (1,248,580 in 2017 / FBI data). 300 million people/1 million attacks. That's a 1 in 300 chance that you'll be the victim of one of those attacks.

---

20 states allow teachers to varying degrees to carry guns on campus. In research covering a 20 year span, there have been zero incidents of gun related attacks in any of the schools where teachers are allowed to carry.

70% of all so called "gun violence" are suicides. The majority of the remaining 30 percent are drug/gang related.

Prior to 1972 Israeli citizens were not allowed to have firearms. Do to the overwhelming number of terrorist attacks, Israel eased up on their gun laws and terrorist attacks went down dramatically.

France has a virtual ban on civilian gun ownership, yet in (1 year) 2015 France had more casualties from mass public shootings (532 total) than America in the 8 years from 2008-2016 (527 total).

Brazil has a homicide rate six times that of America and they have some of the strictest gun laws in the world. Only 2 tenths of 1% of Brazilian adults are legally able to own a gun.

Mexico has some of the strictest gun-control in the world and their murder rate is seven times that of America.

Every single country that has restricted or eliminated its citizens the right to own a gun, has seen an increase in violence.

Good Gun Bad Guy 3

ABOUT THE AUTHOR

Dan Wos is an American Entrepreneur, Author and Musician. Dan is a 2nd Amendment advocate and national speaker on the topic of guns and how we perceive them. He continues to write, and appear on radio and TV across the country.

RESOURCES

WEBSITES

www.goodgunbadguy.com

www.goodgunbadguy.blogspot.com

www.danwos.com

https://twitter.com/Dan_Wos

https://www.facebook.com/janmorganhomepage

http://www.gunowners.org

www.nra.org

www.johnrlott.blogspot.com

www.fbi.gov

www.cdc.gov

On NRATV with Dana Loesch 2019

With Erich Pratt, Gun Rights Policy Conference Phoenix, AZ 2019

With KrisAnne Hall, BamaCarry Event 2018

With Willes Lee (NRA Board Member) 2018

With Beth Alcazar, Associate Editor at USCCA (AKA,The
Phoenix Photo Bomber) at AMMCON 2019 Phoenix, AZ

With Sean Spicer, Northshire Bookstore, Saratoga Springs, NY 2019

With Maj Toure, Gun Rights Policy Conference Phoenix, AZ 2019

With Congresswoman Elise Stefanik, 2018

Good Gun Bad Dog (Apollo)

"There is no such thing as **Gun-Violence,** only **Human-Violence.**"

"Until we can successfully educate the fearful and irrational anti-gun crowd, they will continue to chase whatever ghost they are told to chase."

- Dan Wos
Author, Good Gun Bad Guy

Made in the USA
Middletown, DE
07 December 2019